THIRTEEN LESSONS
IN
CHRISTIAN
DOCTRINE

Copyright © 1968
College Press Publishing Company

Second Printing - November 1970
Third Printing - May 1972
Fourth Printing - April 1973
Fifth Printing - July 1974
Sixth Printing - July 1975
Seventh Printing - June 1977
Eighth Printing - September 1979

Printed and Bound in the
United States of America

All Rights Reserved

International Standard Book Number: 0-89900-136-X

THIRTEEN LESSONS
IN
CHRISTIAN DOCTRINE

Denver Sizemore

College Press, Joplin, Missouri

FOREWORD

The publication of this book brings a forceful and forthright presentation of Christian Doctrine to be appreciated by the general student. Having used these outlines in their earlier form to great advantage in establishing the new convert, I look forward to a continued use of this more detailed and elaborate treatment. Drawing from many years of research and classroom presentation, Mr. Sizemore has put together a concise, coherent, and perceptive work. His explanations, illustrations, and printed texts, enhances the clarity of context and makes more pleasant the study of Christian Doctrine. This treatment will be of mutual advantage to both teacher and student.

Ragon T. Flannery
Administrative Director

Church of Christ Building
and Loan Fund, Inc.

Southern California
Evangelistic Association

TABLE OF CONTENTS

1

Lesson One

GOD

I. Evidence for God's existence:
   A. Bible reveals it.
   B. Reason teaches it.
   C. Supreme intelligence indicates it.
   D. Nature proves it.
   E. Intuition requires it.

II. Names for God.

III. The Nature of God:
   A. His unity—one God.
   B. His holiness.
   C. His love.
   D. His mercy.
   E. His power—omnipotence.
   F. His wisdom—omniscience.
   G. His omnipresence.
   H. His faithfulness.

IV. Knowing and Obeying God.

Is there a God? If so, what is He like? Does he care about us? What does He require of us? These are questions that all men must face. The answer to these will determine the direction and goal of each life.

2

GOD

I. EVIDENCE FOR GOD'S EXISTENCE

A. *The Bible does not attempt to prove the existence of God.* The first statement is: "In the beginning God . . . (Gen. 1:1) It assumes it as a fact and asserts that "The fool hath said in his heart, 'There is no God'." (Psa. 14:1) The Bible states that only a fool, ingnorant of the facts would deny God, and then not openly, but secretly in his heart. The Bible is written on the premise that the evidence for God is so strong that no informed person would deny His existence.

However, to those who will not accept the Bible teaching concerning God, it becomes necessary to examine added proof for His existence. A few evidences will suffice:

B. *Reason teaches it.* The law of cause and effect requires that back of every effect there must be a cause. The world is the effect. What is the cause? Did the world and this universe come into being by change? Did nothing produce something? Or is there a master mind, which we call God, back of it? Reason would teach the latter. The Bible agrees: "For every house is builded by some man; but he that built all things is God." (Heb. 3:4)

C. *Supreme intelligence.* When we see a great house, we know there was a wise architect. When we hear a beautiful song, we know there was a composer. When we look at this earth, we know there was a creator. The earth is said to weigh about 6,570,000,000,000,000,000,000,000 (6 Sextillion, 570 quintillion) tons. Its dimensions: 8,000 miles in diameter and 25,000 miles in circumference. Yet the earth is more accurate in its movements than the finest and most delicate watch. The earth travels over 292,000,000 miles in a year's time as it circles the sun. Yet it does not vary in the length of time it takes for each trip by as much as one second! If it were to vary one-half a second it would make scientific headlines around the world. It has done this for thousands of years! How can this be explained? A wise and powerful God is the most sensible answer.

D. *Nature proves it.* The Psalmist declared: "The heavens declare the glory of God, and the firmament showeth His handiwork." (Psalm 19:1). Paul, in Romans 1:20, adds "For the invisible things of him from the creation of the world are clearly seen, being understood by the things that are made, even his eternal power and Godhead; so that they are without excuse." As we look at the world about us we can be assured there is a God, and that He is powerful and wise. People who reject this evidence are without excuse for their disbelief. Someone has written, "If the word 'God' were

3

LESSONS IN CHRISTIAN DOCTRINE

written upon every blowing leaf, embossed on every passing cloud, engraved on every granite rock, the inductive evidence that God is in the world would be no stronger than it is. When the human intellect thinks in terms of finality with The world as its premise, the 'therefore' of every syllogism will be 'God'. The universe is a big advertising poster spelling 'God'."

E. *Intuition requires it.* Man intuitively recognizes a higher being and desires to worship it. This is true of the most pagan tribes. Paul found this to be true in Athens (Acts 17:23) among the pagan idol worshippers. Where did man obtain this knowledge and concept of a divine being? The animals do not have it. The fact that man alone in all creation is a religious being is evidence that this knowledge was placed within him by his designer, God. The atheist is unable to explain it otherwise.

This skeptical age is rejecting God while wading through an ocean of evidence for Him. It reminds one of the poem by Minot J. Savage:

"Oh, where is the sea?" the fishes cried,
As they swam the crystal clearness through,
"We've heard from old of the ocean's tide,
And we long to look on the waters blue.
The wise ones speak of the infinite sea;
Oh, who can tell us if such there be!"

II. NAMES FOR GOD

The most common name for God in the Old Testament is "Jehovah." This means the "self-existent one." The question is often asked, "Where did God come from?" The answer is that He didn't come from anywhere or anyone. He exists within Himself and always has. With our limitations we find this hard to grasp, but this is one indication that God is unlimited. When Moses asked God for His name in Exodus 3:14, He said, "Thus shalt thou say unto the children of Israel, I AM hath sent me unto you." This is another way of saying Jehovah—"the existing one." This name clearly implies that God is eternal, (Psalm 90:2).

The name "ELOHIM" is applied to God in Gen. 1:1 and elsewhere in the Old Testament. This means "The strong one." This refers to His omnipotent "all-powerful" nature. This is especially used in connection with creation.

"Adon"—meaning "Lord, Master" is often applied to God in the Bible. This indicates His authority over man as well as all creation.

4

GOD

NATURE OF GOD

Physical creation can tell us there is a God. But it remains for the Bible—God's revelation of Himself to tell us what God is like in His person. We list a few of His many attributes.

A. *His unity—One God.* There is but one God. (Duet. 6:4) "Hear, O Israel: The Lord our God is one Lord." The American Standard Version more accurately translates it: "Jehovah our God is one Jehovah." Yet there are three persons in the Godhead—the Father, the Son, and the Holy Spirit. The term "God" is applied to each of these. (I Cor. 8:6; John 1:1; Acts 5:3-4). The term "God" is used here as an expression of deity rather than as a proper name.

This idea of three persons but one God did not seem to disturb the writers of the New Testament. They apparently accepted it by faith realizing the inability of finite man to fully understand the nature of an infinite God. In some respects man is triune like God. Paul describes man as "spirit and soul and body." (I Thess. 5:23) Man is a spirit with a soul and lives in a body. Yet he considers himself as one. This however is not fully understood by any one. If man cannot understand his own nature he should not be surprised at not understanding the nature of God. We accept Him by faith as we do the majority of things in this world.

B. *His Holiness.* This is one of the greatest distinctions between the one true God and gods created by man. The gods that men create are sinful and weak like their creators. A study of Greek Mythology which narrates the sinful natures of the gods on Mt. Olympus will confirm this. Presumably when man creates a god, he does not create one who will condemn him for his sins.

This is not true of Jehovah. While Israel was surrounded by pagan gods of unholy natures, Jehovah thunders from Mount Sinai "Ye shall be holy: for I the Lord your God am holy." (Lev. 19:2) The prophet Isaiah saw in the temple a vision of the Lord with the seraphims crying one to another, "Holy, Holy, Holy, is the Lord of hosts: the whole earth is full of his glory." (Isa. 6:3) The first petition for God in the Model Prayer is "Hallowed be thy name." (Matt. 6:9)

It is the holiness of God that causes him to hate everything that is sinful and evil, and love everything that is pure, and good, and holy. The Psalmist sang to God, "Thou hatest all workers of iniquity." (Psa. 5:5) It is God's perfect holiness that makes it impossible for Him to be tempted by evil, much less to sin. (James 1:13)

5

LESSONS IN CHRISTIAN DOCTRINE

A woman dressed in a white satin dress abhors dirt much more than a ditch digger does. The cleaner one becomes in soul, the more he detests sin. Since God is completely holy, He has a burning hatred of all evil. The destruction of the world by the flood, and the final destruction of the earth by fire are expressions of God's attitude toward sin because of His holiness.

The term "saint" in the New Testament means a "holy one" or one living a holy life. Every child of God who is living a holy life is a saint. As children of a holy God we are caled upon to live like Him. ". . . as children of obedience, not fashioning yourselves according to your former lusts in the time of your ignorance: but like as he who called you is holy, be ye yourselves also holy in all manner of living; because it is written, Ye shall be holy; for I am holy." (I Peter 1:14-16 ASV)

C. *His Love.* This is the supreme attribute of God. "He that loveth not knoweth not God; for God is love." (I John 4:8) Love comes nearer than any other characteristic to describing the nature of God. (cf. Isa. 63:7-9) Love is the matchless motive that sent Jesus to save lost humanity. (Jn. 3:16)

The love of God is seen first in His sending Christ to earth to save man. (I John 4:9-10) His love is also seen in His adopting into the family of God those who obey the Gospel. (I Jn. 3:1) His love is superior to any love man might have. (Romans 5:6-8)

We see God's love in His providential care of all men and especially His care for the redeemed. (Matthew 5:44-48; Romans 8:28).

His repeated forgiveness of our sins comes from His love. King Hezekiah said, "But thou hast in love to my soul delivered it from the pit of corruption: for thou hast cast all my sins behind thy back." (Isaiah 38:17).

God's love for us begets in us love for Him. "We love him, because he first loved us." (I John 4:19). His love also motivates us to love one another. "Beloved, if God so loved us, we ought to love one another." (I John 4:11; cf. John 14:15).

D. *His Mercy.* God's love is the basis of His mercy as seen in John 3:16. Paul further states: "But God, who is rich in mercy, for his great love wherewith he loved us, even when we were dead in sins, hath quickened us together with Christ, (by grace ye are saved;) and hath raised us up together and made us sit together in heavenly places in Christ Jesus: that in the ages to come he might shew the

6

exceeding riches of his grace in his kindness toward us through Christ Jesus." (Eph. 2:4-7).

Three great words are closely associated in the Bible: Love, mercy, and grace. LOVE is the basis of His MERCY, and God extends GRACE (unmerited favor) because He is merciful.

The greatest expression of God's love, mercy, and grace was when Jesus came to atone for our sins. "Herein is love, not that we love God, but that he loved us, and sent his Son to be the propitiation (the atoning sacrifice) for our sins." (I John 4:10). God could have let us die in our sins and He would have been just in doing it. But God chose to be merciful and save us even though we in no way deserved it.

God shows His mercy daily, when He answers our repentant prayers for forgiveness. Our understanding high priest, Jesus, and the throne of grace are always ours "that we may obtain mercy, and find grace to help in time of need." (Heb. 4:16). The Lord is "longsuffering to us-ward, not willing that any should perish, but that all should come to repentance." (II Peter 3:9) How wonderful is His mercy!

E. *His Power — Omnipotence.* God says in Gen. 17:1, "I am the almighty God." The term "Almighty" means there is no limit to His power. In Rev. 19:6, the heavenly host sang, "Alleluia; for the Lord God Omnipotent reigneth." It is this limitless power that enabled God to create the world in the beginning and maintain it today. The miracles of the Bible were performed because of God's power. Men have difficulty believing the Genesis creation story and the Bible miracles because they have rejected the omnipotent God. Jesus said, "With God all things are possible." (Matt. 19:26).

F. *His Wisdom — Omniscience.* Paul sings a hymn of praise to God's wisdom in Rom. 11:33, "O the depth of the riches both of the wisdom and knowledge of God! How unsearchable are his judgments, and his ways past finding out!" God's knowledge and understanding are unlimited. "Great is our Lord, and of great power: his understanding is infinite." (Psa. 147:5).

God's knowledge is so great that it extends to little, insignificant things as well as great facts. Jesus says He sees the sparrow fall, and that the very hairs of our head are all numbered. (Matt. 10:30) John writes, "For if our heart condemn us, God is greater than our heart, and *knoweth all things.*" (I Jn. 3:20).

He knows all about us even to our thoughts. "Thou knowest my downsitting and mine uprising, thou understandest my thought afar off. Thou compassest my path and

7

LESSONS IN CHRISTIAN DOCTRINE

my lying down, and art acquainted with all my ways. For there is not a word in my tongue, but lo, O Lord, thou knowest it altogether." (Psalm 139: 2-4).

G. *His Omnipresence.* Being spirit God can be everywhere. He is always present. Jehovah declares, "Am I a God at hand, saith the Lord, and not a God afar off. Can any hide himself in secret places that I shall not see him? saith the Lord. Do not I fill heaven and earth? saith the Lord." (Jer. 23:23-24). David in Psalms 139:7-10, could think of no place where he could go and be beyond the love and care of God. We are never far from God as Paul told the pagan audience at Mars Hill, (Acts 17:27-28) "That they should seek the Lord, if haply they might feel after him, and find him, though he be not far from every one of us: for in him we live, and move, and have our being . . ."

God is unlimited by time because He is eternal, unlimited in power since He is omnipotent, His omniscience means that he is unlimited in knowledge, and His omnipresence informs us that He is not limited by space. "For Jehovah your God, he is God of gods, and Lord of lords, the great God!" (Deut. 10:17).

H. *His Faithfulness.* "Know therefore that Jehovah thy God, he is God, the faithful God, who keepeth covenant and loving-kindness with them that love him and keep his commandments to a thousand generations." (Deut. 7:9).

In the midst of constant change in every area of life it seems that nothing is stable. All of life seems built on shifting sand. But not so with God! Humbolt the explorer, related his experience with an earthquake in South America. As the earth beneath him rocked like a boat in the water, trees fell, rocks rolled, he felt that nothing was stable or dependable. Then he looked upward. The sun was still there, the sky was undisturbed. How like life that is! The things of this earth do change—God does not. David says: "Of old hast thou laid the foundation of the earth: and the heavens are the work of thy hands. They shall perish, but thou shalt endure: yea, all of them shall wax old like a garment; as a vesture shalt thou change them, and they shall be changed: but thou art the same, and thy years shall have no end." (Psalm 102:25-27).

The faithfulness of God is rooted in His immutability— His unchanging nature. Jehovah says, "For I am the Lord, I change not." . . . (Mal. 3:6) His methods and covenants with men may change, but his principles and character do not. Because He does not change, man can place his trust in every promise He makes. The omnipotence of God further

GOD

assures his faithfulness. Men may not keep promises because they are unable through weakness to carry them out. God can perform anything he promises to do.

The Hebrew writer therefore could say with confidence, "Let us hold fast the profession of our faith without wavering: (for he is *faithful* that promised.") (Heb. 10:23).

KNOWING AND OBEYING GOD

As we consider how great God is, we would agree with God's words in Jer. 9:23-24, "Let not the wise man glory in his wisdom, neither let the mighty man glory in his might. let not the rich man glory in his riches: but let him that glorieth glory in this, that he understandeth and knoweth me, that I am the Lord which exercise lovingkindness, judgment, and righteousness, in the earth: for in these things I delight, saith the Lord."

Man's highest aim in life should be to "Fear God, and keep his commandments: for this is the whole duty of man." (Ecc. 12:13).

QUESTIONS — GOD

TRUE - FALSE

_____ 1. The Bible assumes the existence of God.

_____ 2. For every effect there must be a cause.

_____ 3. There is little evidence from nature to tell us of God.

_____ 4. It is easy to understand that God has always been.

_____ 5. The Christian accepts by faith the nature of God.

_____ 6. Man has no knowledge of God until he reads the Bible.

_____ 7. Omnipresence means unlimited in space.

_____ 8. Immutability refers to God's unchanging nature.

_____ 9. The gods that men create are powerful and holy.

_____ 10. The New Testament teaches that every one is a saint.

9

LESSONS IN CHRISTIAN DOCTRINE

FILL IN THE BLANKS

1. In John 3:16, God's attributes of _____ and _____ _____ are seen.

2. God's faithfulness is assured by His _____ and _____.

3. God's love for us should beget in us a love for _____ and for _____.

4. God's _____ is defined as unmerited favor.

5. God is not tempted by evil because of His _____.

Lesson Two

JESUS, THE CHRIST

I. Jesus, The Son of God.

II. Titles that indicate His work and position.
   A. Jesus, Our Saviour.
   B. Jesus, Our Lord.
   C. Jesus, Our Mediator.
   D. Jesus, Our Prophet.
   E. Jesus, Our High Priest.
   F. Jesus, Our King.

"And thou shalt call His name JESUS; for it is He that shall save His people from their sins." (Matt. 1:21) Thus the angel of the Lord informs Joseph about Jesus, His name and His mission. Jesus is the Greek equivalent for the Hebrew word "Joshua" meaning "Jehovah is salvation." Jesus means "Saviour", aptly describing His work of saving men from their sins. (Luke 19:10)

The title Christ or Messiah means "anointed one." It designates Jesus as the fulfiller of the Messianic hopes of the Jews in the Old Testament. The name Jesus Christ means that He is the Messiah who came to earth to save lost mankind.

I. JESUS, THE SON OF GOD

The logical question that follows is, Who is this Jesus, this Messiah? Many answers have been given. Some of the Jews thought Him to be Mary and Joseph's son. (Mk. 6:3; Matt. 13:55) Others called Him a "deceiver". (Matt. 27:63) Still others thought Him to be a prophet (John 6:14). Some men today say that He is just a man except that He lived a better life than other men.

11

LESSONS IN CHRISTIAN DOCTRINE

What does the Bible say? What did Jesus say? What did the Apostles who knew Him best say?

JOHN THE BAPTIZER SAID JESUS IS THE SON OF GOD. "And I have seen, and have borne witness that this is the Son of God." (John 1:34)

MARK SAID JESUS IS THE SON OF GOD. "The beginning of the Gospel of Jesus Christ, the Son of God." (Mark 1:1)

PETER SAID JESUS IS THE SON OF GOD. "And Simon Peter answered and said, 'Thou art the Christ, the Son of the living God.' " (Matt. 16:16)

PAUL SAID JESUS IS THE SON OF GOD. "God sent forth His Son, made of a woman, made under the law." (Gal. 4:4)

THE ANGEL GABRIEL SAID JESUS IS THE SON OF GOD. ". . . that holy thing which shall be born of thee shall be called the Son of God." (Luke 1:35)

THE DEMONS SAID JESUS IS THE SON OF GOD. "What have we to do with thee, Jesus, thou Son of God . . . ?" (Matt. 8:29)

JESUS SAID HE WAS THE SON OF GOD. "Again the high priest asked Him, and saith unto Him, Art thou the Christ, the Son of the Blessed? And Jesus said, I am." (Mk. 14:62; cf. Matt. 26:64; Jn. 10:36)

The crowning testimony came from the FATHER who said: "This is my beloved Son, in whom I am well pleased." (Matt. 3:17; cf. Matt. 17:5)

A. *Divine powers and honors ascribed to Jesus*. In addition to the above testimony to Christ's deity, He is said to possess powers and honors that belong only to Deity.

1. Christ has the power to create. Throughout the Bible the power to create is attributed to God. (Gen. 1:1; Isa. 48:12-13) Yet in many passages of Scripture the same power is ascribed to Jesus. (John 1:1-3; Eph. 3:8-11; Col. 1:16-17)

2. Christ has power to forgive sins. This is an exclusive power of God. Yet in Luke 5:20-25, Jesus states that He has the power to forgive sins and demonstrates it by healing the paralytic.

3. Christ is a proper object of worship. God alone is to be worshipped. Nevertheless this honor is given to Jesus by the Father. "For the Father judgeth no man, but hath committed all judgment unto the Son; that all men should honor the Son, even as they honor the Father. He that honoreth not the Son, honoreth not the Father who hath sent Him." (John 5:22-23)

These powers and honors are Christ's because He is "the only begotten Son, who is in the bosom of the Father . . ." (John 1:18). When Jesus spoke to the people about God, He never used the term "Our Father". He never classed Himself

12

with other men to indicate equality. (In Matt. 6:9 Jesus uses the term "Our Father", but this was in giving a prayer for the disciples to pray.)

Jesus is not a mere man. He is the only begotten Son of God. He came to earth and lived as a man for a few years. But He is and always has been in a unique sense—God's Son.

II. TITLES THAT INDICATE HIS WORK AND POSITION

One man has said that he counted two hundred fifty-four different titles given for Jesus in the Bible. A diamond has many facets, yet each one will reflect some new and beautiful side of the gem. Like a diamond, one may look at Jesus from any angle or facet of His life and see some new beauty reflecting His greatness and love for man.

In this lesson we will study just a few of these many facets of the Master's life.

A. *Jesus, Our Saviour.* Webster defines Saviour as "one who saves or delivers." This facet of Jesus' life perhaps shines the brightest of all.

The angel told Joseph, "Thou shalt call His name Jesus, for it is He that shall save His people from their sins." (Matt. 1:21). The angel of the Lord told the shepherds on the Judean hillside "there is born to you this day in the city of David a Saviour, who is Christ the Lord." (Luke 2:11). Jesus summarized concisely His mission to earth when He said, "For the Son of man came to seek and to save that which was lost." (Luke 19:10).

Romans 5:6-8 states that while man was weak, unable to save himself; while he was a sinner not deserving salvation, that by the grace and love of God, Christ died to save Him. I Peter 1:18-19 relates that man has been redeemed, bought back and rescued from slavery not with silver or gold, "But with precious blood as of a Lamb without blemish and without spot, even the blood of Christ." (ASV).

Willis R. Hotchkiss, missionary to Africa, searched for many months for a native word that would express the idea of Saviour. One day there was a great commotion in the village. When Mr. Hotchkiss joined the crowd assembled in the square, he found a native, torn and bleeding. He was excitedly telling of his escape from the claws of a tiger. He used a word to describe the one who had saved him.

Immediately Mr. Hotchkiss wrote this word down. The next Sunday he preached on Jesus as Saviour and used this word. As the people crowded around him after the service they said, "Now we *understand* that Jesus died *to save* us

LESSONS IN CHRISTIAN DOCTRINE

from sin and satan. That's what you've been trying to tell us for so many moons."

Mr. Hotchkiss says, "I have dwelt four years practically alone in Africa. I have been 30 times stricken with the fever, three times attacked by lions and several times by rhinoceroses; a number of times ambushed by the natives; for fourteen months I never saw a piece of bread. But let me say to you, I would gladly go through the whole thing again if I could have the joy of again bringing that word 'Saviour' and flashing it into the darkness that enveloped another tribe in Central Africa."

Many false religions offer their followers some hope of salvation through abuse of the body and personal torture. Others by keeping certain moral maxims. Even then the hope is faint. The grand assurance of Christianity is that God in His love toward man saved us, not by works of righteousness which we do, "but according to His mercy He saved us, through the washing of regeneration and the renewing of the Holy Spirit, which He poured out upon us richly through Jesus Christ our Saviour." (Titus 3:5-6, ASV).

Christianity alone has a Saviour! One more reason why we believe it to be the only *true* religion.

B. *Jesus, Our Lord.* No term is more expressive of the faith of the early believers than the term "Lord." Peter proclaimed on Pentecost that the Jews had crucified Jesus but that God had made Him "Both LORD and Christ." (Acts 2:36). In Acts 10:36, Peter says He is "Lord of all."

Paul declares that we are to confess with the mouth "Jesus as LORD." (Romans 10:9 ASV). The believer confesses Jesus as his Saviour, as his Messiah or Christ, but especially as his Lord!! In Phil. 2:9-11, Paul explains that "God highly exalted him (Jesus), and gave unto him the name which is above every name; that in the name of Jesus every knee should bow, of things in heaven and things on earth and things under the earth, and that every tongue should confess that Jesus Christ is LORD, to the glory of God the Father!"

The term Lord indicates the sovereignty of Christ over His followers—the church. (Colossians 1:18). He is the Master, the Christian is His servant. The term Saviour indicates what Christ has done and is doing for the believer. The term Lord reflects what the believer should DO for Christ his Saviour. Many people love to read and hear of what Jesus has done for them. But often they are unconcerned about what Christ expects and requqires of them in return. If Christ is not Lord of All, He will not be our Lord at all! Jesus

14

said, "And why call ye me, Lord, Lord, and do not the things which I say?" (Luke 6:46). This facet of the Lord's life needs emphasizing today.

C. *Jesus, Our Mediator.*

The term mediator suggests one that is a "go-between" two parties. It implies that the two parties are hostile or at variance with each other and this mediator is endeavoring to bring them into harmony and agreement. The scriptures teach that man when in sin is at enmity with God, alienated from Him, without hope.

Christ came and died that He might make peace between God and man, whether Jew or Gentile; "and might reconcile them both in one body unto God through the cross, having slain the enmity thereby." (Eph. 2:16)

Christ died on the cross in order to remove the great barrier between God and man—SIN. By accepting Jesus' proffered forgiveness through the Gospel, man may be reconciled and be at one with God.

Christ alone was qualified to remove this barrier, since He alone was without sin. No one could die for another's sins, while he had sins of his own. It is also true that Jesus alone can be a Mediator between God and man. Paul says "For there is one God, *one mediator* also between God and men, himself man, Christ Jesus, who gave Himself a ransom for all." (I Tim. 2:5) Jesus states, *"no one* cometh unto the Father, but by me." (Jn. 14:6)

A mediator should have knowledge of both sides and be concerned for the welfare of each party. Jesus "existing in the form of God" before He came to earth fully understood God's side. He came to earth that He might know and understand man's side. (Read Heb. 2:17-18; 4:15-16)

Now He is the perfect and *only* Mediator between God and man.

D. *Jesus, Our Prophet.*

When the work of Jesus is viewed in its broad sweep it divides itself generally into three offices which He fulfills—prophet, priest, and king.

The prophet in the Old Testament was a man who spoke forth for God. Amos said he was not a prophet by training, or the son of one but was a herdsman and a dresser of sycamore trees. But "Jehovah took me from following the flock, and Jehovah said unto me, Go, prophesy unto my people Israel. Now therefore hear thou *the word of Jehovah.*" (Amos 7:14-16) The prophets were forthtellers, speaking God's message for the present time and need. They were also foretellers, predicting events yet to come.

15

LESSONS IN CHRISTIAN DOCTRINE

The Old Testament points unmistakably to one great prophet who would come to be God's spokesman on earth. In Deut. 18:15 Moses revealed that "Jehovah thy God will raise up unto thee a prophet from the midst of thee, of thy brethren, like unto me; unto him ye shall hearken." Peter informs us that this prophet was Jesus. (Acts 3:19-26)

Hebrews 1:1-2 states that God had in other times communicated His message to man through many channels, but "hath at the end of these days spoken unto us in His Son." Jesus came to be the divine Teacher and revealer of God's will for man.

As God's prophet Jesus spake authoritatively that the people might know that He spoke for God. "The multitiudes were astonished at His teaching: for He taught them as one having authority, and not as their scribes." (Matt. 7:28-29) Yet He spoke simply and clearly that all men might understand. "The common people heard Him gladly." (Mk. 12:37b) All agreed, even His enemies, "Never man so spake!" (Jn. 7:46)

The prophetic ministry of Jesus was carried on after He returned to heaven by the Holy Spirit whom He sent. Jesus told His disciples the night before He died, "But the Comforter, even the Holy Spirit, whom the Father will send in my name, *he shall teach you all things,* and bring to your remembrance all that I said unto you." (Jn. 14:26)

When we read the New Testament we can accept it with faith and full assurance that it is God's message for us. Jesus, God's great prophet, has said, "My teaching is not mine, but His that sent me." (John 7:16). "I speak the things which I have seen with my Father." (John 8:38).

E. *Jesus, Our High Priest.* A priest was a minister or leader of any religion, whether heathen (Acts 14:13) or Biblical (Matt. 8.4). The high priest was the leader among the priests. In Hebrews Jesus is referred to ten times as our High Priest. Christ is pictured as the True High Priest of which Aaron was a type. All Christians are priests (I Peter 2:9).

His duties as expressed in Hebrews 5:1 were: "For every high priest, being taken from among men, is appointed for men in things pertaining to God, that He may offer both gifts and sacrifices for sins." The function of the high priest under the Mosiac period was to lead in the Temple worship of Jehovah, and to offer sacrifices to God on behalf of the people. Aaron, being human and therefore a sinful high priests had to first offer a sacrifice for his own sins and that of his family (Lev. 16). Then he would enter a second time

16

into the Holy of Holies, sprinkling blood on the Mercy Seat for the sins of Israel. By this act the sins of Israel were rolled forward year by year until Christ should come, "The Lamb of God" to completely take away the sins of the people. (Hebrews 10:1-4)

1. Jesus commissioned as High Priest. In Hebrews 5:4-6, the writer records that Jesus was made a High Priest by God Himself; "And one does not take the honor himself, but he is called by God, just as Aaron was. So also Christ did not exalt Himself to be made high priest, but was appointed by him who said to him, 'Thou art my Son, today I have begotten thee'; as he says also in another place, 'Thou art a priest forever, after the order of Melchizedek.' " (RSV)

David had known this and stated it in Psalm 110:4. We have already stated that Jesus is our Prophet, High Priest, and King. It is interesting to note that Jesus is not a High Priest after the order of Aaron. Aaron was from the tribe of Levi—the priestly tribe. The New Testament writers make much of the fact that Jesus was "of the House and lineage of David," (Luke 2, 4, and 5; cf. Mk. 11:10; Matt. 21:9). How could Jesus be a High Priest and come from the tribe of Judah which was the kingly tribe? The answer is to be found in the fact that Jesus is a High Priest after the order of Melchizedek. (Heb. 6:20; 7:15-17). Melchizedek was the superior of Abraham and both King of Salem and Priest of God Most High. (Hebrews 7:1-4).

2. His Preparation. Jesus' preparation or training to be our great High Priest began when He left the glories of Heaven and came to earth to become one with those He represents. (Phil. 2:5-8).

Hebrews 2:14 reveals that Jesus was a partaker or sharer in "flesh and blood" in the same manner that we are. In Hebrews 4:15, His preparation continues as He is tempted in all points like as we are and yet without sin. A part of His training for this great office is seen in Hebrews 5:8 where we read that He learned obedience by the things which He suffered, thus being made perfect or complete as our High Priest. In order to properly mediate between God and Man, Jesus needed "to be made like unto His brethren that He might become a merciful and faithful High Priest in all things pertaining to God, to make propitiation for the sins of the people. For in that He Himself hath suffered being tempted, He is able to succor them that are tempted." (Hebrews 2:17, 18).

Apart from having sin, there is nothing in human experience that is unknown to Him. Today as our faithful and merciful High Priest, He ministers before God on behalf of His people who are compassed by sin and infirmity. (Heb. 4:15-16; Rom. 8:33-34)

3. His Offering:

When Aaron made atonement for the sins of Israel under the Old Covenant, he used the blood of bulls and goats for a sacrifice. But when Jesus our High Priest, offered His sacrifice to God, He offered Himself. (Heb. 9:11-12) "But Christ having come a high priest of the good things to come through the greater and more perfect tabernacle, not made with hands, that is to say, not of this creation, nor yet through the blood of goats and calves, but through his own blood, entered in once for all into the holy place, having obtained eternal redemption." (ASV).

From the scriptures we note these facts:

a. The Tabernacle in which Christ offered His sacrifice was not a tent in the wilderness or a Temple in Jerusalem. The Atonement was made not in the Holy of Holies in Jerusalem but in Heaven itself before the presence of God. (Heb. 9:24)

b. His altar of sacrifice was not the brazen one in the Temple court, but a rude cross on Golgotha's Hill.

c. His sacrifice was not the blood of goats and calves but rather His own "precious blood, as a Lamb without blemish and without spot." (I Peter 1:19) He is the sacrifice and the sacrificer. (Jn. 10:17-18)

d. The effect of His sacrifice: The effect of Aaron's sacrifice on the Day of Atonement merely made a remembrance year by year—it did not take away sin. (Heb. 10:4)

However, when Jesus offered His sacrifice, He did not need to offer Himself year by year, "else must he often have suffered since the foundation of the world: but now once at the end of the ages hath he been manifested *to put away sin* by the sacrifice of Himself." (Heb. 9:26). Jesus offered once for all the perfect sacrifice that brought to an end animal sacrifice and put away sin forever, having made possible eternal redemption through His blood.

F. *Jesus, Our King.*

1. *Jesus predicted to be a King.* The third great office of Christ that of being King was prophesied by Jeremiah, "Behold, the days come, saith Jehovah, that I will raise unto David a righteous Branch, and he shall reign as King, and deal wisely, and shall execute justice and righteousness in the land." (Jeremiah 23:5; cf. Zechariah 6:13).

His kingship came from God but through the lineage of King David. Gabriel tells Mary "He shall be great, and shall be called the Son of the Most High: and the Lord God shall

18

give unto him the throne of his father David." (Luke 1:32).
God had promised David that one would come from his seed
that would establish a kingdom that would last forever. (II
Sam. 7:12-13). This is fulfilled in Jesus.

2. *Christ claimed to be a King.* After His baptism, He
began preaching that the Kingdom of heaven was at hand. In
Matthew 16:28, Jesus predicted "there are some of them that
stand here, who shall in no wise taste of death, till they see
the Son of man coming in his kingdom." When Pilate asked
Jesus "Art thou the King of the Jews?" He said, "Thou
sayest." This is quivalent to "yes." (Luke 23:3).

3. *Nature of His kingdom.* Jesus said His kingdom was
not of this world. In John 18:36 Jesus informs Pilate "My
kingdom is not of this world: if my kingdom were of this
world, then would my servants fight, that I should not be
delivered to the Jews: but now is my kingdom not from
hence."

Jesus' Kingdom is a spiritual kingdom. (cf. Rom. 14:17;
Heb. 1:8, 9). Christ is indeed a King. He is King of truth;
King of salvation; King of peace; King of righteousness.
His rule is over the hearts of men for the great purpose of
saving their souls.

4. The length of His rule. Gabriel told Mary "He shall
reign over the house of Jacob for ever; and of His kingdom
there shall be no end." (Luke 1:33). Peter urges all Christians
to be diligent in making their calling and election sure. "For
thus shall be richly supplied unto you the entrance into the
eternal kingdom of our Lord and Saviour Jesus Christ. (II
Peter 1:11). Christ is in His mediatorial reign now as He
seeks to redeem lost mankind. He shall continue to reign in
eternity. Then we shall see the many diadems upon His
head, and shall know that He is truly "King of Kings and Lord
of Lords." (Revelation 19:12, 16).

QUESTIONS — JESUS, THE CHRIST

TRUE - FALSE

_____ 1. The name Jesus means Saviour.

_____ 2. Jesus did not claim to be the Son of God.

_____ 3. The term Lord tells what Jesus has done for us.

_____ 4. A mediator is one who reconciles two parties.

19

———— 5. A prophet is one who speaks God's message to man.

———— 6. Christ is a prophet like Elijah.

———— 7. The main task of the high priest was to offer sacrifices for sin.

———— 8. Jesus was a high priest after the order of Aaron.

———— 9. Prophets in the Old Testament were both forthtellers and foretellers.

————10. Jesus shall be King forever.

FILL IN THE BLANKS

1. List two powers that God has that Christ also has.

   a. _____.

   b. _____.

2. List three contrasts between Aaron's sacrifice for sin and Jesus' sacrifice for sin.

   a. _____.

   b. _____.

   c. _____.

3. Is God reconciled to man or is man reconciled to God? (II Cor. 5:18-20, Eph. 2:14-18)

   _____

   _____

   _____

Lesson Three

THE BIBLE

I. Names for the Bible.

II. The Origin of the Bible.
   A. What the Bible says about its origin.
   B. Evidences for the divine origin of the Bible.
      1. Fulfilled prophecy.
      2. Its wonderful unity.
      3. Logical proof.

III. The Value of the Bible.
   A. Its value to the lost.
   B. Its value to the saved.

IV. How to Read and Understand the Bible.

V. The Sacredness of the Word.

The Bible is the most remarkable book in the world. Thomas Carlyle said, "I call the Bible, apart from all theories about it, one of the greatest things ever written with pen. A noble book! All man's book!"

It is by far the world's best seller. Two million copies have been sold each year for the past 100 years. It has been translated into over 1,000 languages and dialects. This is more than any other book.

Alexander Campbell wrote:

LESSONS IN CHRISTIAN DOCTRINE

The Bible is to the intellectual and moral world of men what the sun is to the planets in our system —the foundation and source of light and life, spiritual and eternal. There is not a spiritual idea in the whole human race that is not drawn from the Bible. As soon will the philosophers find an independent sunbeam in nature, as the theologian a spiritual conception in man, independent of the ONE BEST BOOK." (Christian System, page 3)

I. NAMES FOR THE BIBLE

The word Bible itself simply means "book." Many religions have their collection of sacred writings, sometimes spoken of as their bibles. To the Christian the Bible means the collection of the Scriptures of the Old Testament and New Testament recognized and used as the basis and authority of the Christian faith. The Bible uses other terms to identify itself.

A. *Word of God.* "And for this cause we also thank God without ceasing, that, when ye received from us the word of the message, even the word of God, ye accepted it not as the word of men, but as it is in truth, the word of God, which also worketh in you that believe." (I Thessalonians 2:13) Peter states that we are begotten through "the Word of God, which liveth and abideth." (I Peter 1:23) This identifies the Bible as the message or word which has come from God.

B. *Living Oracles or Oracles of God.* Stephen speaks of the law given on Mount Sinai as "living oracles". (Acts 7:38) An oracle is a message handed down from a divine being or source. This name indicates that this message from Jehovah is a living message from a living God. Paul calls the Bible "The Oracles of God." (Romans 3:2) Moses told the children of Israel to keep the Commandments of God and to teach their children to observe them also. "For it is no vain thing for you; *because it is your life,* and through this thing ye shall prolong your days in the land, whither ye go over the Jordan to possess it." (Deut. 32:47 cf. Hebrews 4:12)

C. *The Holy Scriptures.* Paul refers to the Old Testament writings as the "Holy Scriptures". (Romans 1:2) This simply means "sacred writings" which is the expression used in II Timothy 3:15. The Word scripture itself means "writing." This is the common term used for the Old Testament books by our Lord and His Apostles. (Matt. 21:42; Mark 14:49; Luke 24:32; John 5:39; Acts 18:24; Romans 15:4)

22

THE BIBLE

II. THE ORIGIN OF THE BIBLE

A. *What the Bible says as to its origin.*

In a court of law the most important evidence as to the author of a will is what the will actually says itself. If the will states that John Brown is its author it takes considerable evidence to prove it otherwise. This principle holds true also in determining who is the real author of the Bible. Let us examine what the Bible says as to its author.

1. *Old Testament*—Several hundred times the Old Testament writers use such expressions as "Thus saith the Lord," "Jehovah said," etc. (Exodus 24:12, 25:1; Ezekiel 5:5, 11) David speaks in II Samuel 23:2, "The Spirit of the Lord spake by me, and his word was in my tongue." Jeremiah describes his call to prophesy like this: "And Jehovah said unto me, Behold I have put my words in thy mouth." (Jeremiah 1:9)

The Apostle Paul speaking of the Old Testament scriptures said regarding their inspiration: "All scripture is given by inspiration of God, and is profitable for doctrine, for reproof, for correction, for instruction in righteousness: That the man of God may be perfect, throughly furnished unto all good works." (II Timothy 3:16, 17)

The Apostle Peter informs us that the prophets in the Old Testament did not create their own message, "For no prophecy ever came by the will of man: but men spake from God, being moved by the Holy Spirit." (II Peter 1:21 ASV) It is a well known fact that Jesus and the Apostles always considered the Old Testament to be a revelation from God.

2. *New Testament*—Not only did the Old Testament writers declare that their message came from God but the New Testament authors also claimed that their message was from God. Paul says in Galatians 1:11, 12, "But I certify you, brethren, that the gospel which was preached of me is not after man. For I neither received it of man, neither was I taught it, but by the revelation of Jesus Christ."

Peter speaks of Paul's writing as "scripture" when he says, "As also in all his epistles, speaking in them of these things; in which are some things hard to be understood, which they that are unlearned and unstable wrest, as they do also the *other scriptures,* unto their own destruction." (II Peter 3:16) The word scripture as used here indicates a special body of writing which was regarded as divinely inspired. The expression "other scriptures" shows that Peter places Paul's writing on a par with the Old Testament. Jesus had told His Apostles that the Holy Spirit would enable them to recall all that He had ever taught them. The Holy Spirit would also teach them many other things. (John 14:26, cf. Matt. 10:19, 20). Paul commended the brethren at Thessalonica because they had received his message "not as the word of men, but as it is in truth, the *Word of God.*" (I Thessalonians 2:13)

The unanimous testimony of the Bible is that its author is God. It was written down by men who were inspired by the Holy Spirit.

B. *Other Evidence for the Divine Origin of the Bible.*

1. *Fulfilled prophecy*—One of the great proofs of the inspiration of the Bible is fulfilled prophecy. This is predicting accurately a future event that comes to pass hundreds of years later. When this is done it is strong evidence that the prophet possesses supernatural power. Occasionally some one might make a lucky guess but when scores of prophecies are accurately fulfilled, the possibility of chance is removed.

(a) Prophecies concerning Jesus—Below is a partial list of prophecies concerning Jesus and their fulfillment in the New Testament.

	Prophecy	*Fulfillment*
1. Place of Jesus' birth	Micah 5:2	Luke 2:1-7
2. His forerunner foretold	Isa. 40:3; Malachi 4:5	Matt. 3:1-3; 11:11-14
3. His betrayal by Judas	Psalm 41:9	John 13:18; Lk. 22:47,48
4. He died with transgressors	Isa. 53:9,12	Luke 23:33
5. Not a bone to be broken	Psalm 34:20	John 19:31-37
6. Buried by a Rich man	Isaiah 53:9	Matt. 27:57-60
7. His Resurrection foretold	Psalm 16:10	Matt. 28:1-6

These and many other prophecies in the Old Testament bear eloquent testimony to a divine author of the Bible.

2. *Its wonderful unity*—The Bible was written over a period of 1,500 years on three different continents by some 40 human writers. Its human writers by occupation were sheepherders and kings; farmers and doctors. The Bible was written in three different languages, and covers in its 66 separate books, every subject imaginable. Yet, it is essentially one book! How can this be possible?

This unity many be illustrated by a great orchestra. It may be composed of a 100 musicians with a score of different types of instruments. Yet when they play, there is one grand harmony. The reason being that there is one master mind, the conductor who directs and controls all the musicians, as they play. God made His great oratorio to play for more than a 1000 years and when one musician became silent, another took up the strain and it was all one grand symphony —the theme was never lost and when the last strain dies away it is seen that through all these glorious movements and melodies there has been one grand theme.

Did each musician compose his own music and play it as he chose? Or was there one composer and director behind it all? The real conclusion is that God is the true author of the Bible and that He directed each writer as He inspired him by the Holy Spirit. This is the answer to the unity of the Bible.

3. *Logical proof*—John Wesley had a very brief but interesting way of proving the Bible to be from God. He said the Bible must be the invention of good men or angels; bad men or devils, or of God.

(a) It could not be the invention of good men or angels; for they neither would nor could make a book, and tell lies all the time they were writing it, saying, 'Thus saith the Lord,' when it was their own invention.

(b) It could not be the invention of bad men or devils; for they would not make a book which commands all duty, forbids all sin, and condemns their souls to hell to all eternity.

(c) Therefore, he drew this conclusion, that the Bible must be given by divine inspiration.

III. THE VALUE OF THE BIBLE

How important is the Bible to the Christian? What is its value to the lost? We who believe it, know that it is of the greatest importance to both.

A. *Its Value to the Lost.* The Scriptures state:

(1) We are begotten by the Word. "Being born again, not of corruptible seed, but of incorruptible, by the word of God, which liveth and abideth forever." (I Peter 1:23) James says, "Of his own will begat he us with the word of truth, that we should be a kind of first fruits of his creatures." (James 1:18)

(2) We are saved by the Word. "Wherefore lay apart all filthiness and superfluity of naughtiness, and receive with meekness the engrafted word, which is able to save your souls." (James 1:21)

(3) Faith comes through the Word. "So then faith cometh by hearing, and hearing by the word of God." (Romans 10:17)

We know that Christ is the one who saves us. The Bible, however, is the source of our knowledge of Christ and His saving power. Without the Word there would be no knowledge of His redeming love and hence there would be no faith or obedience on man's part. This is why the Bible says we are saved through the Word. It is the channel that God uses to bring us to Christ.

B. *Its Value to the Saved.* To the Christian, the Bible is indispensable. There are many ways in which the scriptures are valuable to the life of a Christian.

(1) As a means of Spiritual growth. "As new born babes, desire the sincere milk of the Word, that ye may grow thereby." (I Peter 2:2) The Bible is to the spiritual man what the food is to the physical body. It is food to his soul. Jesus said "man is not to live by bread alone, but by every word that proceedeth out of the mouth of God." (Matt. 4:4) A neglect of the study of the Word makes spiritual weaklings. Paul told the Ephesian elders, "And now, brethren, I commend you to God, and to the word of his grace, which is able *to build you up,* and to give you an inheritance among all them which are sanctified." (Acts 20:32)

(a) By the Word of God, believers are cleansed from the defilement of sin. Jesus told His apostles "now ye are clean through the Word which I have spoken unto you." (John 15:3) We know that it is the blood of Christ which cleanseth us from all sin. (I John 1:7; Hebrews 9:14) It is through the Word, however, (Knowledge of and obedience to it) that we are brought to that blood. The Psalmist posed this question and gave this answer "Wherewithal shall a young man cleanse his way? By taking heed thereto according to thy Word." (Psalm 119:9)

The Word is the means whereby we are kept clean and set apart or sanctified for God's use. Jesus prayed the Father, "Sanctify them through thy truth; thy Word is truth." (John 17:17)

One man has said, "This Book will keep you from sin, or sin will keep you from this Book."

(b) By the Word of God, Christians are able to meet the attacks of satan. When satan tempted Jesus in the wilderness, our Lord parried every thrust by the use of the Word of God. (cf. Matt. 4:1-11) Paul told the Ephesians, "Put on the whole armour of God, that ye may be able to stand against the wiles of the devil . . . And take the helmet of salvation, and the sword of the Spirit, which is the word of God." (Ephesians 6:11, 17) The Bible is the Christian's sword in this spiritual battle against sin. The Psalmist also recognized this truth when he said, "Thy word have I hid in mine heart, that I might not sin against thee." (Psalm 119:11)

(c) A thorough knowledge of the Word gives confidence and courage to the soul winner. A man who professed to be an unbeliever had embarrassed many local preachers with his infidel arguments. An evangelist came to town to lead a gospel meeting. This man went to the revival to "do up" the evangelist with every argument. The unbeliever advanced. The evangelist answered each question with a "Thus saith the Lord." Frustrated and embarrassed, he left the meeting. The next day, a friend asked him how he fared in the debate.

He replied, "Not so well. But I did not go up there to argue with God Almighty."

IV. HOW TO READ AND UNDERSTAND THE BIBLE

Jehovah is a God of Wisdom. His revelation is a Book of knowledge. God always invites man to come now "and let us reason together saith the Lord." (Isaiah 1:18a) This being true, the Word of God should be approached with the same intelligence and thoughtfulness with which one would approache any book of knowledge.

Here are a few principles of correct study that will make the Bible more intelligible and meaningful.

1. Determine *who* is speaking. It may be God or Satan or Balaam's mule or the fool. It is very important to have a correct understanding to know who is speaking the particular statement.

2. To *whom* is the Word speaking. Is the Word speaking to the Christian or the alien sinner? The meaning may be entirely different depending on which it is.

3. Of *what* does it speak? What is the content—What goes before and what follows this particular passage? This simple bit of knowledge will clear up many otherwise difficult scriptures.

4. *When* does it speak? Ask, Is this passage written for those living in the Patriarchal age, or the Mosiac age, or the Christian age? God has dealt with His people in different ways under each of these periods. It is important to the Christian that he follow God's instructions for him today. This last rule is most important.

V. THE SACREDNESS OF THE WORD

Since the Bible is a revelation from God, having been written by Holy Spirit inspired men, it should be handled with the utmost reverence. Moses told Israel, "Now therefore hearken, O Israel, unto the statutes and unto the judgments, which I teach you, for to do them, that ye may live, and go in and possess the land which the Lord God of your fathers giveth you. Ye shall not add unto the word which I command you, neither shall ye diminish ought from it, that ye may keep the commandments of the Lord your God which I command you." (Deut. 4:12)

A similar idea is in the last admonition in the Bible. "I testify unto every man that heareth the words of the prophecy of this book, If any man shall add unto them, God shal addl unto him the plagues which are written in this book: and if any man shall take away from the words of the book of this prophecy, God shall take away his part from the tree of life, and out of the holy city which are written in this book." (Revelation 22:18, 19)

Since the Bible is God's Word, man to his own peril adds to it or takes from it or neglects it. When all men shall stand before the great white throne this Word will be one of the Books that will judge them at that time. If we obey God's Word, it will save us. If we disobey, it will condemn us. (Colossians 3:16) May we heed the Word of Paul and let the Word of Christ dwell in us richly. (Colossians 3:16a)

QUESTIONS — THE BIBLE

FILL IN THE BLANKS

1. The word Bible means _____.

2. An oracle is _____

_____

3. What is the most important evidence in establishing the Authorship of a document?

_____

_____

4. The Bible was written over a period of _____

years on _____ continents by some _____ human writers.

5. John Wesley thought there were only five sources for the Bible. List them.

THE BIBLE

a. _____ b. _____ c. _____

d. _____ e. _____

6. List three (3) blessings the word brings to the believer.

a. _____

b. _____

c. _____

7. The Word brings what blessings to the lost?

a. _____

b. _____

c. _____

8. Give four (4) rules for understanding the Bible.

a. _____

b. _____

c. _____

d. _____

Lesson Four

THE CHURCH

I. **What is the Church?**
   A. Meaning of the Word—Church.
   B. Local and general significance of the word.

II. **The Beginning of the Church.**
   A. Predictions of the coming Church.
   B. Establishment of the Church or Kingdom.
   C. Evidence from prophecy.

III. **The Founder of the Church.**

IV. **The Foundation of the Church.**

V. **The Government of the Church.**

VI. **Names for the Church.**
   A. The "Church".
   B. The Church of God.
   C. House of God.
   D. Temple of God.

I. WHAT IS THE CHURCH?

A. *Meaning of the word—Church.* The word that Jesus chose to describe His people was an ancient Greek word— "Ecclesia". Our word ecclesiastical comes from it, which means "relating to the Church." The word originally designated the regular assembly of the citizens in a free city-state. The citizens were "called out" by the herald to transact the public business. Hence, the word means "the called out ones."

THE CHURCH

The Church, therefore, is composed of those who have been called out of sin into righteousness—out of the world into the Church. Peter expresses this thought in I Peter 2:9, "But ye are an elect race, a royal priesthood, a holy nation, a people for God's own possession, that ye may show forth the excellencies of him who *called you out of darkness into his marvellous light.*" The Christian has been called through the gospel to come out from the world (II Cor. 6:17, 18) and into Christ for the purpose of transacting business for God.

Stephen referred to the children of Israel in the Old Testament as God's assembly or congregation in the wilderness. (Acts 7:38). Israel too, had been called out of Egypt to become God's chosen people and to do His will. This is a type of the Lord's Church today.

B. *Local and general significance of the word.* In the New Testament the term Church had both a local and a general significance. It referred both to the individual congregation and to the worldwide community of God's people.

In Acts 5:11 it speaks of the Church in Jerusalem. The term Church in Acts 9:31, however, refers to many congregations when Luke says, "So the Church throughout all Judea and Galilee and Samaria had peace, being edified . . ." Often Paul would address small groups of Christians meeting in a home. (Romans 16:3-5; Colossians 4:15; Philemon 2). Yet Paul speaks of the Church in its broad comprehensive sense in I Corinthians 10:32 and I Timothy 3:15. Each congregation was the Church in its community. It was, however, an integral part of the entire fellowship of Christians. Groups of Christians may be separated b ygeography but still be one in Christ and His Church. Perhaps Thomas Campbell gave as good a definition of the Church as anyone, when he said;

> The Church of Christ, upon earth is essentially, intentionally, and constitutionally one; consisting of all those in every place that profess their faith in Christ and obedience to Him in all things according to the Scriptures, and that manifest the same by their tempers and conduct, and of none else; as none else can be truly and properly called Christians.[1]

II. THE BEGINNING OF THE CHURCH

A. *Predictions of the coming Church.* The first mention of the word Church in the Bible is Matthew 16:18. Peter had confessed Jesus as the Christ and as the Son of God. Jesus

---

1. Richardson, Robert, *Memoirs of Alexander Campbell*, (Cincinnati: Standard Pub. Co., 1890, Vol. I.), Page 258.

LESSONS IN CHRISTIAN DOCTRINE

blessed Peter and said, "Upon this rock I will build my Church." By the use of the future tense, Jesus clearly indicates that the Church had not yet been established. Jesus continues His thought regarding the Church when He says to Peter, "I wil lgive unto thee the keys of the kingdom of heaven; and whatsoever thou shalt bind on earth shall be bound in heaven; and whatsoever thou shalt loose on earth shall be loosed in heaven." (Matt. 16:19). It is evident from the use of the term Church in verse 18 and the term "Kingdom of heaven" in verse 19 that these terms are interchangeable. The terms "Church" and "Kingdom" are also used in a similar way in Colossians 1:13 where Paul speaks of "the Kingdom of His dear Son." And then in verse 18, without a break in thought, describes the same entity as "the body, the Church." These terms denote the same body of people.

The establishment of Christ's kingdom or Church had been mentioned before this discussion with Peter. John the Baptist announced the coming kingdom when he cried, "Repent ye; for the Kingdom of heaven is at hand". (Matt. 3:2). The expression "at hand" signifies that it was near. Jesus, soon afterwards, preached, "Repent ye; for the Kingdom of heaven is at hand." (Matt. 4:17). The Lord told His Apostles "that there be some of them that stand here, which shall not taste of death, till they have seen the Kingdom of God come with power." (Mark 9:1). The Kingdom was to be established with power during the lifetime of the Apostles.

B. *The Establishment of the Church or Kingdom.* During Christ's earthly ministry, He did not establish the Church. After His resurrection, the disciples asked Him, "Lord, doest thou at this time restore the Kingdom to Israel?" (Acts 1:6). Jesus replied, "It is not for you to know times or seasons, which the Father hath set within his own authority. But ye shall receive power, when the Holy Spirit is come upon you: and ye shall be my witnesses both in Jerusalem and in all Judea and Samaria, and unto the uttermost part of the earth." (Acts 1:7, 8). He also commanded them to "tarry ye in the city of Jerusalem, until ye be endued with power from on high." (Luke 24:49). The fulfillment of these promises regarding the Holy Spirit and the establishment of the kingdom took place on the first Pentecost after Christ's resurrection. Read Acts 2:1-42. At that time the Apostles were baptized in the Holy Spirit and received the promised power. Peter preached the first gospel sermon and about 3,000 believed in Christ as their Lord and Messiah, repented of sin and were baptized into Christ. (Acts 2:36-41). These were the terms of admission into the Lord's Church. Every reference to the Church after the Day of Pentecost shows that it is already in existence. (cf. Acts 5:11; 8:1). Peter settled the question as to the beginning of the Church in Acts 11:15 when he speaks of Pentecost as being "the beginning".

C. *Evidence from prophecy.* The evidence here presented from the New Testament as to the beginning of the Church is confirmed by prophecy. Isaiah, in 2:1-3, predicted that in the last or latter days, which refers to the Christian age, that the mountain of the Lord's house would be established. It would be great and all nations would flow into it. Then he gives this significant prophecy, "For out of Zion shall go forth the law and the word of Jehovah from Jerusalem."

God had given the law of Moses at Mt. Sinai but the gospel of His son was to go forth from Jerusalem. Jesus corroborates this prophecy in Luke 24:46, 47 when he says, "Thus it is written, that the Christ should suffer, and rise again from the dead the third day; and that repentance and remission of sins should be preached in his name unto all the nations, beginning from Jerusalem."

Christ's church or kingdom was established on the Day of Pentecost following Christ's resurrection and ascension.

III. THE FOUNDER OF THE CHURCH

The Church is not a human structure like a political or social institution. It is a divine organism. It has a divine founder and a divine head.

Jesus had told the Apostles *"I* will build *my* Church." It is His Church. He is the builder. He is the head of the Church. (Colossians 1:18). Paul calls it "the church of the living God." (I Timothy 3:15). The Church is the bride of Christ which has been saved and sanctified by Him for union with Himself. (Ephesians 5:25ff). The Church is also referred to as the body of Christ. (Ephesians 1:22, 23; 4:12; Colossians 1:18). As the body, it is the fulness of Christ, who Himself fills all in all. (Ephesians 1:23).

The Church belongs to Christ also because He purchased it with His own precious blood. Paul instructs the Ephesian elders "to feed the Church of the Lord which He purchased with His own blood." (Acts 20:28; cf. I Peter 1:18-19).

IV. THE FOUNDATION OF THE CHURCH

A divine church with a divine head, needs also a divine foundation. This it has! When Peter confessed Jesus as the Messiah and the Son of God, Jesus replied, "upon this rock I will build my church; and the gates of hades shall not

33

LESSONS IN CHRISTIAN DOCTRINE

prevail against it." (Matt. 16:18). Throughout the scripture, Jesus is referred to as a rock. For example, in Isaiah 28:16 God says, "Behold, I lay in Zion for a foundation a stone, a tried stone, a precious corner stone of sure foundation. . . ." Peter quotes this in I Peter 2:6ff, and applies it to Christ. Jesus is referred to as the stone which was cast aside by human builders but God made Him the head of the corner. (Acts 4:11, 12). Paul settles the question of the foundation of the church when he says, "other foundation can no man lay than that which is laid, which is Jesus Christ." (I Cor. 3:11). Christ is the founder of the Church. He is the foundation.

V. THE GOVERNMENT OF THE CHURCH

Every properly functioning organization or organism must have some form of government. The church is no exception. When the church is considered universally, its form of government is an absolute monarchy. When it is viewed from the standpoint of a local congregation, it has a limited power of self-government.

a. Jesus Christ is the head and absolute authority of the Church. "And He put *all things* in subjection under His feet, and gave Him to be head over *all things* to the church." (Ephesians 1:22).

"But speaking the truth in love, may grow up in all things into him, who is the head, even Christ." (Ephesians 4:15)

"For the husband is the head of the wife, as Christ also is *the head* of the Church, being Himself the saviour of the body." (Ephesians 5:23).

"And He is the head of the body, the Church: who is the beginning, the firstborn from the dead; that in all things he might have the pre-eminence." (Colossians 1:18; cf. 2:10).

(1) As the supreme authority in the Church, Jesus has *all* power. "And Jesus came to them and spake unto them, saying, 'All authority hath been given unto me in heaven and on earth." (Matthew 28:18).

(2) As head of the church Christ has all *legislative* power. Christ has the power to enact laws to govern His Church and its activities.[1]

He has enacted the following laws and they are incorporated in the constitution:

1. Qualification of citizenship. John 14:6; Mark 16:16;
2. Qualifications of officers of the kingdom. I Tim. 3:1-13; Titus 1:5-9;

1. DeWelt, Don, *The Church and the Bible.* COLLEGE PRESS, Joplin, Missouri.

34

THE CHURCH

3. Duties of citizens. Matt. 5:3 to 7:27; I Peter 2:21;
4. Duties of officers. II Tim. 4:2; I Peter 5:2; Acts 6:1-6;
5. Laws of finance. I Cor. 9:1-13; 16:1-2; I Tim. 5:17-18;
6. Laws of discipline. I Cor. 5:1-13; I Thess. 5:12; I Tim. 5:20;
7. Laws for the reinstatement of the backslider. Acts 8:18-24; II Cor. 2:5-11.

Having this power, one can see the full significance of Jesus' command to His Apostles when in the great commission He said to go and teach and baptize, "Teaching them to observe *all things* whatsoever I commanded you. . . ." (Matt. 28:20) Christ's promise to be with the Church depended upon its obedience to this command.

b. Self-government in the local church. Since the church is composed of human beings, Christ has granted to man limited powers of self-government.

(1) The nature of this self-government. This power is democratic. The membership of the local church is the final authority in matters of self-government. This is seen in such references as Acts 6:35; 11:29, 30; I Cor. 16:3.

This power is exercised through the elders who are the rulers and overseers of the people. They are chosen by the church and lead and rule on behalf of the Church. (cf. I Peter 5:1-5) (For qualifications for elders, see I Timothy 3:1-7 and Titus 1:5-9).

(2) The limitations of this power of self-government. There are definite limitations placed upon the church in the area of self-government. The church's authority to make rules and decisions are limited to matters of opinion and expediency where the scripture has given no definite instructons. For example: The number of elders or deacons the church should select; what kind of a building does the church need; etc. These are matters of importance in the work of the kingdom but there is no "thus saith the Lord" to guide the church. These are areas that Christ has left to human judgment. Even in these areas such decisions should be made in harmony with the spirit and teaching of Christ. W. L. Hayden in his book, *Church Polity*, makes this observation on the subject of self-government:

On what occasion and for what purposes are Christians authorized to vote?

They are not to vote on questions of faith, piety, or morality. Truth is not to be settled by a vote, nor is any divine institution respecting the worship or

35

LESSONS IN CHRISTIAN DOCTRINE

morality of the Christian Church to be decided by a majority. These are matters of revelation, of divine authority, and are to be regulated by a 'Thus saith the Lord,' and not by a 'thus saith the majority.' But in all matters not of faith, piety or morality, in all matters of expediency, there is no other way of deciding but by a vote of the brotherhood.[1]

VI. NAMES FOR THE CHURCH

A. *The "Church."* This is the most often used designation for the Church in the New Testament. Sometimes it is used with the location of the church. For example: "The church throughout all Judea and Galilee and Samaria" (Acts 9:31) or "The Church of the Thessalonians." (II Thess. 1:1). The use of this term without any qualifying phrase indicates the uniqueness of the church. There was nothing else like it in society. There was only one. Christ built only one. The church might be extended over many countries and many continents but it was still "The Church." All Christians were members of this one body. (I Cor. 1:2).

B. *The Church of God.* The next most often used term was the "Church of God," or "Churches of God." (II Cor. 1:1). This name indicates the planner and originator of the Church. It also indicates ownership because the Church belongs to God as well as to Christ.

C. *House of God.* I Timothy 3:15. This name presents the Church as a family. It reminds us that God dwells in His Church and He is Father of all. Jesus also dwells with us and is somewhat like our elder brother. Romans 8:17 reminds us that as children of God we are heirs of God and joint-heirs with Christ. Galatians 3:26,27 reveals how we become sons of God. "For ye are all sons of God, through faith, in Christ Jesus for as many of you as were baptized into Christ did put on Christ."

D. *Temple of God.* I Corinthians 3:16, 17. This name describes the worship feature of the Church. God dwells in His holy temple the Church and is worshipped there. Peter says that Christians "as living stones, are built up a spiritual house, to be a holy priesthood, to offer up spiritual sacrifices, acceptable to God through Jesus Christ." (I Peter 2:5). The Church then is a spiritual temple made up of living stones. (cf. Ephesians 2:19-22). God dwells in each believer through the Holy Spirit which is given to every obedient believer. (Acts 2:38). If the believer is faithful to Christ, the head,

1. DeWelt, Don, *The Church and the Bible.* COLLEGE PRESS, Joplin, Missouri.

THE CHURCH

then some day he will see Him personally as He is. (I John 3:2). In that day God will dwell with His people and be their God. (Revelation 21:3). This is the grand purpose and goal for the church.

QUESTIONS — THE CHURCH

TRUE - FALSE

_____ 1. Christ's Kingdom is spiritual rather than temporal.

_____ 2. The Church and the Kingdom are different bodies.

_____ 3. Isaiah foretold that the Kingdom would be established in Zion.

_____ 4. The term "Church" always refers to the local congregation.

_____ 5. Faith is the only requirement for admission to the Lord's Church.

_____ 6. The Kingdom was established at the Passover.

_____ 7. The Church was started by John the Baptist.

_____ 8. The word "ecclesia" originally referred to an assembly of Greek citizens.

_____ 9. All Christians are members of Christ's church.

_____10. A person can be saved without being a member of Christ's Church.

FILL IN THE BLANKS

1. The government of the Church in its universal sense is an

   _____.: the local church however has

   some _____.

2. In what areas of life does the church lack the authority to vote or make rules?

   _____

   _____

3. List two names for the church and give the significance of each.

   _____

   _____

37

Lesson Five

FAITH

I. The use of the term "Faith" in the New Testament.
   A. Faith—used as a term for Christianity.
   B. Faith—descriptive of the life of the Christian.
   C. Faith—as applied to the alien sinner.

II. What is Faith?

III. How do we obtain faith?
   A. Christian faith is produced in a similar way as any other faith.
   B. Faith results from an acceptance of testimony or evidence.

IV. The Relation of faith to obedience.
   A. The obedience of faith.
   B. Obedience is simply faith in action.

V. The benefits of faith.
   A. It is essential in order to receive all of God's blessings.
   B. Some specific benefits of faith.
      1. Secures salvation for man.
      2. Faith pleases God.
      3. Faith brings peace to the heart of the Christian.
      4. Faith lifts our minds and vision to see as God sees and to think thoughts after Him.

FAITH

I. THE USE OF THE TERM "FAITH" IN THE NEW TESTAMENT

A. *Faith—used as a term for Christianity.* One use of the term faith is to identify the body of truth in which the believer trusts or as another term for Christianity. Jude writes "contend earnestly for the faith which was once for all delivered unto the saints". (Jude 3, ASV) Galatians 1:23 "He that once persecuted us now preacheth the faith of which he once made havoc." In Acts 13:8, Luke records that Elymas withstood Paul and Barnabas "seeking to turn aside the proconsul from the faith." In these passages, as well as many others that might be cited, the word "Faith" is used in its broad sense as a synonym for Christianity.

B. *Faith—descriptive of the life of the Christian.* Romans 1:17 "The righteous shall live by faith". I Thessalonians 1:3, Paul writes, "Remembering without ceasing your work of faith and labor of love and patience of hope in our Lord Jesus Christ." II Corinthians 5:7 "For we walk by faith, not by sight." In these scriptures it should be noted that the Christian lives by faith, works by faith, and walks by faith. The Christian truly lives by faith.

C. *Faith—as applied to the alien sinner.* In order to become a Christian, a sinner must have faith or as it is usually expressed believe in Jesus. "He saith unto them, But who say ye that I am? And Simon Peter answered and said, Thou art the Christ, the Son of the living God." (Matt. 16:15, 16) Paul told the Philippian jailor when he asked the way to salvation: "Believe on the Lord Jesus, and thou shalt be saved, thou and thy house." (Acts 16:31, ASV) Jesus and Paul both commanded faith or belief in Christ as an essential act in becoming a Christian. Let us now examine this faith that is so essential to one's salvation.

II. WHAT IS FAITH?

Hebrews 11:1 "Now faith is the substance of things hoped for, the evidence of things not seen." (KJV) The author defines faith as the "substance" or "guaranty" or "foundation" of things hoped for. It is also the "evidence" or "conviction" or "demonstration" of things not seen.

Faith used in an objective sense is the evidence or guaranty on which the Christian's hope is founded. Used in a subjective sense faith is the "assurance" of things hoped for, and the "conviction" of things not seen. Such assurance or reliance enables the believer to treat the future as though it were the present and the invisible as seen. It is not complete knowledge which one day we shall have but it is that firm assurance that keeps one faithful to the end. Chapter 11 of Hebrews amply shows that true faith as illustrated in Abraham, Moses, Rahab, and others was simply a reliance upon God whom they believed to be trustworthy. Another word which perhaps describes the nature of faith more correctly is the word trust. Faith as used in a general sense may mean simply an acceptance of certain facts or principles as being true. For example, one may believe that George Washington lived but there would be no element of trust in him as a person. Christian faith not only is persuaded of certain facts concerning Christ, but there is the added element of trust in Him as Lord and Saviour. The example of Abraham's faith given in Romans 4:20, 21 illustrates this element of trust. "He (Abraham) wavered not through unbelief, but waxed strong through faith, giving glory to God, and being fully assured that what he had promised, he was able also to perform." Abraham was "strong through faith" because he was "fully assured" that God would fulfill His promise and give him a son. He trusted God so completely, that he believed that if he killed Isaac according to God's command, that God would bring him back to life. (Hebrews 11:17-19).

Robert Richardson states that Alexander Campbell considered the word

'trust' or 'confidence' to substantially express the meaning of the term faith. This simple and comprehensive view was that which Mr. Campbell, in his subsequent religious history, himself adopted, and continued to advocate during his entire life. Amidst his numerous controversies, indeed, he was often obliged, in contending against the popular errors upon the subject, to insist upon the absolute necessity of evidence, and to assert, most truthfully, that where there was no evidence, there could be no faith; yet he ever regarded true faith in Christ as implying a willingness to submit to his authority, and as consisting in a heartfelt, personal trust in Him as the Son of God and the appointed Saviour of mankind.[1]

III. HOW DO WE OBTAIN FAITH?

Many people view anything religious as mysterious. In fact, the more mysterious it appears the more it appeals to

---

1. Richardson, Robert. *Memoirs of Alexander Campbell*, Vol. I., Standard Publishing Company, Cincinnati, Ohio, 1890., pp. 177, 178.

some people. There are always some aspects of faith that man can not fully understand, but in the main the how in which faith is produced in man's heart is a rational and intelligent process, which brings us to our first thought and that is:

A. *Christian faith is produced in a similar way as any other faith.* For example, how is faith in any historical character produced? It is produced by evidence and testimony that is convincing to the mind. We believe that George Washington lived because of the many books written about him, monuments built to him, and other evidence that he lived. How may one be led to believe in or trust a doctor? Evidently he must have received testimony and evidence to generate such faith and confidence.

Faith in Christ is produced in a similar fashion. The Christian accepts as true the abundant evidence in the Bible that Christ lived and is the Messiah and Son of God as He claimed to be. God appeals to the mind of man in a sensible and intelligent manner.

B. *Faith results from an acceptance of testimony or evidence.* The scriptures very clearly indicate that faith is produced by the acceptance of evidence concerning Christ.

"For if ye believe Moses, ye would believe me; for he wrote of me. But if ye believe not his writings, how shall ye believe my words?" (John 5:46, 47)

"Many other signs therefore did Jesus in the presence of the disciples, which are not written in this book: *but these are written, that ye may believe that Jesus is the Christ, the Son of God;* and that believing ye may have life in his name." (John 20:30-31)

"And when there had been much questioning, Peter rose up, and said unto them, Brethren, ye know that a good while ago God made choice among you, that by my mouth the Gentiles should hear the word of the gospel and believe." (Acts 15:7)

These passages make it perfectly clear that Christian faith, like all other faith, must rest on testimony. Paul in Romans 10:16, 17 makes it crystal clear how faith is produced. "But they have not all obeyed the gospel. For Esaias saith, Lord, who hath believed our report? So then faith cometh by hearing, and hearing by the word of God." That faith is a result of testimony, is proven both by the voice of reason and the voice of inspiration.

D. L. Moody is reported as saying that in his early life as a minister, he prayed often that God would give him faith. One day he was reading Romans 10:17, "Faith cometh by

41

hearing . . . the Word of God." Suddenly it dawned upon him that he had been seeking faith in the wrong way. He now realized that God had already told him how to obtain faith. Mr. Moody began to search the word of God diligently, reading God's gracious promises, and striving to accept them. As he read what God had done for Abraham, Moses, David, and others, his confidence in God increased. He concluded that God was the same God now as then. The more he read and filled his mind with the evidence of God's faithfulness, the greater his confidence grew in the promises of God. Thus his faith was increased in complete accord with the way God had promised that it should be.

IV. THE RELATION OF FAITH TO OBEDIENCE

Many times people are confused about the exact relation of faith and obedience. Some feel that there is a conflict between the two. However, a more careful study of the scriptures will indicate that instead of faith and obedience being two separate actions, they are really two parts of one whole.

A. *The obedience of faith.* Paul frequently uses the expression "the obedience of faith". Speaking of Christ in Romans 1:5, Paul says: "By whom we have received grace and apostleship, for obedience to the faith among all nations for his name." (cf. Romans 16:26) Acts 6:7 says, "And a great company of the priests were obedient to the faith." (ASV) What is meant by "the obedience of faith"? The obedience of faith is the obedience which faith produces, or which springs out of faith. Paul is asserting that the gospel is to be preached to bring about obedience that is produced by faith.

1. Two kinds of obedience. There are at least two kinds of obedience in the world. One is an obedience produced by divine faith. The other comes from human reason. One kind of obedience is from God. The other is of man. Man may act from a number of influences or motives. The principle that influences man to act is important. To illustrate, a man may be honest in business because it pays. He may not know or care that God expects him to be honest. He does it because it is good business practice. This would be obedience because of human reason.

Christian obedience may appeal to man's reason but generally does not. There is a reason for this. God desires to know whether we obey Him because of faith and love or whether we obey for some other motive. In all ages God has chosen certain acts which clearly demonstrate man's faith in

God. For example, as far as Eve could see, here was no good reason why she should not eat the forbidden fruit. It was good for food, it was pleasant to the eyes, and it was desirable to make her wise. Therefore, the only motive for not eating was that God had said not to eat it. When she ate the fruit it was a clear case of disobedience.

Today, God has required a similar act of obedience to test our faith. This is the act of Christian baptism. Many people will say, well, I do not see any connection between the act of baptism and my acceptance with God. From a rational standpoint, this is true. There is no way by human reason to explain how baptism is a part of one becoming a Christian, except that Christ says so. Mark 16:16, Jesus says, "He that believeth and is baptized shall be saved." Peter in Acts 2:38 told the 3,000 "repent, and be baptized every one of you in the name of Jesus Christ for the remission of sins, and ye shall receive the gift of the Holy Ghost." When one submits to the act of baptism he does so for the one reason that Christ has commanded it. This is a test of his faith in Christ. It is a test of his love for Christ. Jesus said, "If you love me, keep my commandments." (Jn. 14:15) It is a test of his obedience to Christ.

B. *Obedience is simply faith in action.* This is what James meant when he said that faith, if it is not expressed in obedience or action, is not true faith. Even the demons believe that Jesus is, but their faith never results in obedience. (James 2:14-26) He reminds us that Abraham proved his faith when through obedience he offered Isaac. Obedience is not something a man does in addition or apart from his faith, but rather it is his faith in action. A man does not have true faith unless it does lead him to obedience. Proper understanding of this will also settle any question as to whether a man is saved by faith alone or by obedience alone. He is saved by both. To illustrate, the question could be asked, "Which blade of the scissors does the cutting of the cloth?" The truth is that it takes both blades. In order to obtain salvation, we must use both the blade of faith and the blade of obedience. They can not be separated.

V. THE BENEFITS OF FAITH

The importance of faith can not be exaggerated, since it is the highest principle in the Christian life.

A. *It is essential in order to receive all of God's blessings.* In all ages, God has saved man and blessed him on the principle of faith. Ephesians 2:8 says, "By grace have ye been saved through faith." Grace is the one word that summarizes

LESSONS IN CHRISTIAN DOCTRINE

the great principle upon which God blesses man. It is because of God's love and mercy that He extents all of His benefits to man through grace. The one possible receptive attitude that enables man to receive the blessings of God, is faith. It is the key that opens the door to the treasure chest of heaven.
  B. *Some specific benefits of faith are:*
  1. It secures salvation for man. Peter speaking of the conversion of the Gentiles says, "He (God) made no distinction between us and them, cleansing their hearts by faith." (Acts 15:9) In Acts 10:43 Peter says, "To him (Jesus) bear all the prophets witness, that through his name everyone that believeth on Him shall receive remission of sins." Faith is the response of man to the extended salvation of God.
  As stated before, when the scriptures speak of being saved by faith, it is understood that that faith is expressend in obedience. As proof, Peter in his first epistle, chapter 1, verse 22 says, "seeing ye have purified your souls in your obedience to the truth unto unfeigned love of the brethren." (cf. Romans 6:17, 18)
  2. Faith pleases God. Hebrews 11:6 (ASV), "And without faith it is impossible to be well-pleasing unto him; for he that cometh to God must believe that he is, and that he is a rewarder of them that seek after him." Perhaps the greatest insult that man gives to God, is to doubt His word. Jesus rebuked His disciples for this weakness more often than for any other fault. To refuse or fail to trust the promises of God, is an insult to His love, His grace, and His power to bless man. The Hebrew writer says it is "impossible" to please God without faith.
  3. Faith brings peace to the heart of the Christian. Jesus told His sorrowing Apostles, when He was about to leave them, "Let not your heart be troubled: believe in God, believe also in Me." (John 14:1) Comfort for their sorrowing and fearful hearts would be found in a genuine faith in Christ and God.
  Jesus gives the solution for all fear and worry in Matt. 6:25-34. In simple terms, the solution is a child-like trust in the goodness, love, and power of God. Elizabeth Cheney has summarized this thought in her poem.

OVERHEARD IN AN ORCHARD

Said the Robin to the Sparrow,
  "I should really like to know
Why these anxious human beings
  Rush about and worry so."

44

FAITH

Said the Sparrow to the Robin,
"Friend, I think that it must be
That they have no heavenly Father
Such as cares for you and me."

4. Faith not only brings the above benefits but it also lifts our minds and vision to see as God sees and to think God's thoughts after Him. Ely V. Zollars states this most eloquently.

It should be noted, in this connection, that faith in its various uses covers a very large field. It unlocks the door of the past and pulls aside the curtain of the future. The knowledge therefore, that it gives us is much wider than that which comes through the physical sense, and herein man is lifted infinitely above the plane of the animal. If we were confined in our knowledge to the evidence furnished by these senses, our field would be very much circumscribed. The natural eye and ear can know but a small world. Aided by the microscope and telescope we may have a larger world, but still it is very limited, but by the eye of faith, we can lay hold of that which we have never seen, and can never see with the eye of sense, and thus dwell amidst the beauties that never fade."[1]

QUESTIONS — FAITH

TRUE - FALSE

_____ 1. In Hebrews 11:1 faith is defined as "the substance of things hoped for, the evidence of things not seen."

_____ 2. Faith comes by a direct revelation from heaven.

_____ 3. The New Testament teaches degrees of faith. (See Matt. 8:26; 15:28)

_____ 4. Demons have no faith in Christ.

_____ 5. It is good to have faith but it is not a necessity.

_____ 6. Baptism is a good work a Christian does.

1. Zollars, Ely V., *The Great Salvation.* (Cincinnati: The Standard Publishing Company), page 95-96.

_____ 7. Baptism is an act of obedience expressing faith in Christ.

FILL IN THE BLANKS

1. The term faith is used in what three ways?

   a. _____

   b. _____

   c. _____

2. Alexander Campbell considered that the words_____

   _____ or _____ clearly express the meaning of the word faith.

3. A person may obey for two motives. What are they?

   a. _____

   b. _____

   c. _____

4. List three benefits of faith.

   a. _____

   b. _____

   c. _____

REPENTANCE

Lesson Six

REPENTANCE

I. What is repentance?
   A. Definition of Repentance.
   B. Repentance illustrated.

II. What repentance is not.
   A. Repentance should not be confounded with sorrow.
   B. Repentance is also distinct from reformation.
   C. Repentance should not be confused with fear.

III. Motives which lead to repentance.
   A. The goodness or love of God.
   B. Sorrow for sin.
   C. Fear of judgment.

IV. Restitution and its relationship to repentance.

V. The necessity of repentance.
   A. Repentance, necessary to the alien sinner.
   B. Repentance is also essential for the Christian.

VI. Some hindrances to repentance.
   A. The natural pride of the heart, hinders repentance.
   B. The influence of sinful corrupt desires is another hindrance.
   C. Procrastination is one of the greatest hindrances to repentance.

47

The call to repentance appears early in the Bible. Peter calls Noah "a preacher of righteousness (II Peter 2:5). Though not directly stated, Noah surely preached repentance to the people of his day in an effort to save them from the flood.

The prophets were continually pleading with Israel to repent of their sins and turn to God (Joel 2:12-14; Ezekiel 33:11). John the Baptist came preaching in the wilderness of Judea "Repent ye; for the kingdom of heaven is at hand." (Matthew 3:2). When Jesus began His earthly ministry, He came into Galilee preaching the Gospel of God and saying, "The time is fulfilled, and the kingdom of God is at hand: Repent ye, and believe the gospel". (Mark 1:15)

The message of God is the same in the Christian age. On Pentecost the apostle Peter commanded the people to repent and be baptized in the name of Jesus in order to receive the remission of sins and the gift of the Holy Spirit. (Acts 2:38)

In Jesus' message to the seven churches of Asia (Revelation 2 and 3), he stressed the doctrine of repentance. Eight times in these two chapters, he uses the words repent or repentance. Repentance was a prime need in Bible times. It is even more needful today for those inside as well as outside the Church of our Lord.

I. WHAT IS REPENTANCE?

A. *Definition of Repentance.* The Greek word translated repentance in the New Testament is "Metanoia". This term means "to have another mind" or "To change the mind." The person who repents changes his mind with regard to sin. It is equivalent to the Old Testament word "turn". Thayer's definition of "Metanoia" is: "To change one's mind for the better, heartily to amend with abhorrence of one's past sins." (Thayer's Greek Lexicon, p. 405.)

Professor J. W. McGarvey defined repentance as: "Repentance is a change of will (or mind) caused by a sorrow for sin and leading to a reformation of life." (Commentary on Acts, page 61).

In these definitions should be noted these three steps: (a) Repentance is a change of the mind or will; (b) this change is produced by a sorrow for sins; (c) and leads to a change in conduct and life.

B. *Repentance illustrated.* True repentance is illustrated in the Corinthian church as seen in II Corinthians 7. Paul had rebuked them severely for their sins in the I Corinthian letter. He later wrote in II Corinthians 7:8-9 that he rejoiced,

REPENTANCE

not that they were made sorry by his admonishing but rather "that ye were made sorry unto repentance." He continues, "For godly sorrow worketh repentance (or leads to repentance) unto salvation. . . ." Godly sorrow had preceded and led to their repentance or change of mind. Salvation had followed and was a result of their repentance.

The story of the prodigal son or lost boy in Luke 15 is a good illustration of repentance. The young man's sin is seen in his willful rejection of his Father's authority and home. This willfulness led him into a far country. Here he "wasted his substance with riotous living" (Luke 15:13). We see the depth of his sin when through lack of money, friends, and food, he stooped to the position of feeding swine.

His repentance began when he came to the true realization of his position. Jesus said "when he came to himself" (Luke 15:17). This would indicate that a man in sin is out of his mind! He is not thinking clearly. The young man realized that he had made a mess of his life and that he was lower than the lowest servant in his father's house. This brought him to the first step toward repentance, that is a sorrow for sin. The sorrow for sin led to new resolutions. He said "I will arise and go to my father" (Luke 15:18). He had changed his mind about sin. He now had rejected it and was sorry for it and realized the awful price he paid for the pleasure of sinning for a season. He changed his mind about his father and the father's house. This is the second phase toward repentance.

In order for his repentance to be complete, however, there must be a "change" and "reformation" of life. The young man could have sat there in the hog pen for the rest of his life with his sorrow and his new resolution and never truly repented. His repentance was complete, when Jesus says "and he arose and came to his father" (Luke 15:20).

Here we see illustrated in this story the three elements of repentance: a change of mind caused by a sorrow for sin which in turn led to a reformation of life.

II. WHAT REPENTANCE IS NOT

Having seen by definition and illustration what repentance is, we now turn to the negative side to further understand repentance by showing what it is not.

A. *Repentance should not be confounded with sorrow.* Paul clearly states, "That godly sorrow worketh repentance to salvation. . . ." (II Cor. 7:10). Again he says "Now I rejoice, not that ye were made sorry, but that ye sorrowed to repentance" (II Cor. 7:9). A sorrow for sin is a definite

49

antecedent or motive that leads to repentance, but it in itself is not repentance. They are related like cause and effect. The effect is the change of mind, the cause is the sorrow for sin. One may be sorry for the consequences of sin without being sorry for the sin itself. Most prisoners are sorry for their sins—sorry they were caught! Only when one is genuinely sorry for the sin itself, regardless of the consequences, will this sorrow lead to a forsaking of the sin.

B. *Repentance is also distinct from reformation.* In Matthew 3:8, John told the Pharisees "Bring forth therefore fruit worthy of repentance." He was calling on them to show by their changed life and righteous deeds, that they had truly repented. This reformation of life is a result of repentance, not the repentance itself. It would be possible for a man to reform or even quit doing some evil things, without repenting of them. A man may quit drinking to keep from dying without truly repenting of the sin of drunkenness. Circumstances may lead a man to change his actions when there has been no true change of mind in respect to the sinful life. Reformation then, is the fruit of repentance.

C. *Repentance should not be confused with fear.* It is true that fear of judgment is one motive that· leads to repentance. Fear alone, however, is not repentance.

When Paul preached to Felix, in Acts 24:25, he reasoned of righteousness and self-control and the judgment to come. When Felix heard Paul describe righteousness, which he, Felix, did not have, self-control, which he did not exercise, and the judgment, for which he was not prepared, he was terrified. He answered, "Go thy way for this time; and when I have a convenient season, I will call thee unto me" (Acts 24:25). After Paul had left, and his fear had subsided, Felix gave no evidence of a change of mind or a reformation of life. Many men thinking they were dying have fearfully and tearfully claimed to have repented, but upon recovery, very few ever exhibit a life that would indicate they had repented. Fear is not repentance.

III. MOTIVES WHICH LEAD TO REPENTANCE

The scriptures teach that there are certain motives, "activating forces," that move a person to repentance. The first and perhaps the most important motive that leads a person to repentance is:

A. *The goodness or love of God.* Paul writes in Romans 2:4 "Or despisest thou the riches of his goodness and forbearance and longsuffering, not knowing that the goodness of God leadeth thee to repentance?" John reminds us in I

REPENTANCE

John 4:19 "We love him, because he first loved us." The greatest motivating power in the world is love. It was love that sent Jesus to earth to make possible man's salvation. When a man fully understands the love of God and of Christ, that was demonstrated at Calvary, this becomes the moving force to bring him to repentance.

B. *Sorrow for sin.* We learn from II Cor. 7:10 "For godly sorrow worketh repentance unto salvation, a repentance which bringeth no regret: but the sorrow of the world worketh death." When a man realizes how sin hurts God, his loved ones, and friends; when he recognizes what sin does to him— he's sorry! This leads him to repent.

Paul reminds us also in this scripture, that there are two kinds of sorrow: one godly, and the other worldly. The former brings salvation but the latter brings death.

Peter and Judas illustrate these two kinds of sorrow. Both men had sinned against their Master. When Peter fully realized his sin by the look of the Master and the crowing of the cock, the Bible says "He went out, and wept bitterly" (Matt. 26:75). However, on the resurrection morning, Peter was the first Apostle to enter the empty tomb. For the rest of his life, he continued to follow the steps of the Master. His change of mind was genuine because it lead to a change in his life. He came humbly back to the Master. There Christ forgave him and sent him out to preach.

Judas betrayed the Master. However, by morning, he realized the gravity of his action. The Bible says that he repented himself and brought back the 30 pieces of silver to the chief priests and said, "I have sinned in that I betrayed innocent blood." (Matt. 27:4). We can see from this that Judas had changed his mind. It would certainly indicate a sorrow for his sin. His repentance, though, was not genuine. The word for the repentance of Judas is not "Metanoia". It is another Greek word, "Metamelomai," which signifies a feeling of concern or regret. This feeling of regret may result in repentance or it may degenerate into mere remorse. Judas was sorry for what was happening to the Master. He evidently had not planned for Him to be condemned. He was sorry that his plans had gone awry. He does not seem to have been sorry for the sin itself, because he did not return to the Master to obtain forgiveness and salvation, but he obtained a rope and hanged himself.

Peter had a godly sorrow for sin. It brought him salvation. Judas' sorrow was a worldly sort that led to death.

C. *Fear of judgment.* When Paul addressed the philosophers on Mars Hill in Athens, he reminded them that before

Christ came, God had overlooked their ignorance, but now that Christ had come and salvation was available to all men, he said that God "Commandeth all men every where to repent" (Acts 17:30, KJ). The motive that he gives to move them to repentance is the prospect of the judgment of God. He said, "Inasmuch as he hath appointed a day in which he will judge the world in righteousness by the man whom he hath ordained; whereof he hath given assurance unto all men, in that he hath raised him from the dead" (Acts 17:31). The fear of judgment is not really the highest motive for repentance but sometimes it is very effecive. Often the heart becomes so encrusted with sin that it takes the heavy artillery of God's judgment to blast it away so that the love of God may reach the heart.

It is likely in most cases that God uses all three motives to bring man to repentance.

IV. RESTITUTION AND ITS RELATIONSHIP TO REPENTANCE

Restitution is the act of making amends for the wrongs one has done. The Bible indicates that once a man has repented that he should try to correct or amend as far as humanly possible the wrong he has done.

John told the Pharisees, who came to hear him preach to "bring forth therefore fruit worthy of repentance" (Matt. 3:8). John insisted that there must be some evidence or "fruit" that would indicate a change in thinking and action. (See Acts 26:20)

Zacchaeus understood this principle of restitution. After his encounter with the Master, he said "Behold, Lord, the half of my goods I give to the poor; and if I have wrongfully exacted aught of any man, I restore fourfold" (Luke 19:8). When Jesus heard this and saw the evidence of repentance he said "Today is salvation come to this house, forasmuch as he also is a son of Abraham" (Luke 19:9).

Some years ago a man lived in my home community, who was prone to petty larceny. He would pick up a neighbors shovel or rake, or a window pane that he needed. He stole nothing major, but yet he was guilty of stealing.

During a revival he yielded his life to the Lord. The scoffing unbelievers in the community made great sport of his actions next day. They gleefully told how that he spent most of the day carrying back hoes, shovels, window panes, etc., to his neighbors. They thought this to be very funny. It should be noted, however, that no one questioned the repentance of the new convert. One shovel carried back, in an effort

REPENTANCE

to amend one's past sins would be more eloquent testimony to the genuineness of his repentance than a dozen sermons would.

V. THE NECESSITY OF REPENTANCE

When Jesus gave the Great Commission, He said that "repentance and remission of sins should be preached in His name unto all the nations, beginning from Jerusalem." (Luke 24:47). Jesus told the Jews "Except ye repent, ye shall all in like manner perish" (Luke 13:3). Paul informed the philosophers of Athens that God at one time had overlooked their ignorance and idolatry, "but now he commandeth all men that they should all everywhere repent" (Acts 17:30). Repentance is so important that it is one of the primary acts which stands between man and destruction. One of the reasons for God's long suffering and patience with man is that He is not willing that any should perish, but that all repent and be saved. (II Peter 3:9).

A. *Repentance, Necessary to the alien sinner.* The great purpose of the Gospel is to save man from sin, but before it will save him, his heart must be purified from sin. Acts 2:38 tells us that this is accomplished when individuals responding from faith, repent and forsake sin and are baptized into Christ. God has only promised to forgive man when he is willing to repent and forsake his sins. Before an alien sinner can claim the promise of salvation he must, through faith, repent and obey the Gospel. Peter confirms this in I Peter 1:22, where he states that souls are purified through "obedience to the truth."

B. *Repentance is also essential for the Christian.* What does a Christian do to obtain forgiveness of sin after he has come into Christ? Peter answers this question in the 8th chapter of Acts. Simon had believed in Christ and had been baptized into Christ. However, temptation became too strong for him and he sinned. After rebuking him severely, for his sin, Peter tells him how to obtain forgiveness. He said, "Repent, therefore of this thy wickedness, and pray the Lord, if perhaps the thought of thy heart shall be forgiven thee" (Acts 8:22). Two steps then are necessary: repentance and a prayer for forgiveness. It is evident that to pray without repentance would be a useless exercise. But prayer, coupled with repentance will save from sin.

VI. SOME HINDRANCES TO REPENTANCE

A. *The natural pride of the heart, hinders repentance.* Stephen severely rebuked the Sanhedrin just before they stoned him by saying, "Ye stiffnecked and uncircumcised in

53

LESSONS IN CHRISTIAN DOCTRINE

heart and ears, ye do always resist the Holy Spirit: as your fathers did, so do ye" (Acts 7:51). Man is naturally proud. It is difficult for any man to acknowledge that he has sinned or done wrong. Pride prompts one to cling to things that are wrong rather than admitting his sin and weakness. It takes true moral heroism to humbly admit wrongs and forsake them. Humility is truly a priceless virtue! Jesus said, "Except ye turn and become as little chlidren, ye shall in no wise enter into the kingdom of heaven" (Matthew 18:3). It took considerable humility for the prodigal to "swallow his pride", go back home, and admit to his father and his older brother, that he had sinned. Many will be lost in eternity because pride hindered their repentance.

B. *The influence of sinful corrupt desires is another hindrance.*

The necessary consequence of repentance, involving the giving up of sensual gratifications, appetites, sordid pleasures, lust, gross forms of sin, all must be subdued or given up. Here is a surrender many can not make. The drunkard may weep over his sin, yet his burning appetite keeps him from the deliberate purpose to abandon his habits of dissipation. Sorrow suggests repentance, but appetite makes a powerful counter appeal, and the man hesitates and is lost.[1]

C. *Procrastination is one of the greatest hindrances to repentance.* Many people come to the end of life with out repentance not because they intended to but, like Felix, were always looking for a convenient season. The scriptures cry out against this, as they remind us that today is the day of salvation. Heaven is too wonderful, hell is too awful, and eternity is too long to put off repentance.

QUESTIONS - REPENTANCE

FILL IN THE BLANKS

1. Write McGarvey's definition of Repentance.

_____

_____

1. Zollars, Ely V., *The Great Salvation.* (Cincinnati: The Standard Publishing Company, 1805, page 121).

REPENTANCE

2. Sorrow is to Repentance what _____._____ is to

_____ _____.

3. _____ is the fruit or result of repentance.

4. List Three (3) hindrances to repentance.

   a. _____

   b. _____

   c. _____

5. Paul lists two (2) kinds of sorrow in II Corinthians 7:10.

   They are: _____ and _____

6. Peter states that a Christian is to _____ and

   _____in order to receive forgiveness. (Acts
   8:22)

TRUE - FALSE

_____ 1. A good definition for repentance is "a sorrow
for sin."

_____ 2. Restitution means to make amends for one's
wrongs.

_____ 3. In the Bible, love of God is the only motive for
repentance.

_____ 4. Humility is not needed in order to repent.

_____ 5. Jeremiah indicates that repentance was the chief
message of the prophets. (Jeremiah 25:4, 5)

Lesson Seven

BAPTISM

I. The authority for baptism.

II. The method or action of baptism
   A. Plain statements of Scripture
      1. Water
      2. Much water
      3. Going to the water
      4. Going down into the water
      5. Coming up out of the water
   B. The symbolism of baptism
      1. Baptism is a picture of a burial and a resurrection
      2. Baptism, a picture of a birth
   C. The meaning of the Greek word.

III. The person to be baptized
   A. A person must be a beliver in Christ
   B. A person is not only to be a believer but he should be a penitent believer.
   C. Though not specifically commanded, there seems to have been a public confession of Christ preceding baptism in the New Testament.

IV. The Proper purpose for baptism
   A. In order to be saved
   B. For the remission of sins
   C. For washing away of sin
   D. Baptism into Christ

BAPTISM

Jesus said, "For what is a man profited, if he shall gain the whole world, and lose his own soul? or what shall a man give in exchange for his soul?" (Matt. 16:26). Any subject that relates to the salvation of one's soul is an important subject, and needs careful study. Since Jesus said, "He that believeth and is baptized shall be saved," (Mark 16:16) baptism in water is such a subject.

Jesus considered baptism important enough to walk some 60 to 70 miles from Nazareth to be baptized by John in the Jordan River to set us an example. In eight clear examples of conversion in the book of Acts, baptism is specifically mentioned. Certainly our Lord and the Apostles believed this to be a vital part of obedience. We must consider it significant also.

Our aim in this lesson is to study the teaching of the New Testament concerning baptism. We will try to answer these questions: (1) Who commanded the act of baptism? (2) What is the method or action of baptism? (3) Who is to be baptized? (4) What is the purpose of baptism?

I. THE AUTHORITY FOR BAPTISM

One way of determining the importance of any act or doctrine, is by the source of authority for it. After Jesus' resurrection, He gave the Apostles the Great Commission. He said, "Go ye therefore and make disciples of (or teach) all the nations, baptizing them in the name of the Father and of the Son and of the Holy Spirit" (Matt. 28:19, 20). The command came from the Lord Jesus and was to be done in the name of the Father and of the Son and of the Holy Spirit.

The expression, "in the name of . . ." usually means "by the authority of. . . ." When a policeman arrests a criminal "In the name of the law" he means "by the authority of the law." The act of baptism was authorized by the heavenly Father, the Lord Jesus, and the Holy Spirit. There can be no higher authority than this.

In Acts 2:38, Peter commanded baptism "in the name of Jesus Christ." Since God has delegated all authority to Jesus, during this age (Matt. 28:18), it would not be necessary to repeat each time, the name of the Father, and the Holy Spirit, because to do it in the name of Jesus would be doing it by the authority of all three.

II. THE METHOD OR ACTION OF BAPTISM

In this present time, there has been much discussion regarding the proper form or action of baptism. What is done, physically speaking, when one is baptized? This question can be easily answered by the New Testament. We shall use three lines of evidence in determining the action of baptism.

A. *Plain statements of Scripture.* The Bible was written so that ordinary people could understand it. God desires that everyone be saved. The things that a man needs to do to be saved are written in simple language. Let us examine the Scriptures to see what baptism is.

The Bible teaches that the act of baptism requires:

1. Water. (Acts 10:46f, 47). "Then Peter answered, Can any man forbid the water, that these should not be baptized?" Matthew 3:13 records that Jesus came to the Jordan river to be baptized by John. Water then is essential to the act of baptism.

2. Much water. (John 3:23). "And John also was baptizing in Aenon near to Salim, because there was much water there: and they came, and were baptized." It does not say John was *preaching* there because there was "much water". but rather he was *baptizing* there because there was "much water." Baptism then requires much water.

3. Going to the water. Invariably the person to be baptized in the New Testament went to the water. It never mentions water being brought to the candidate. It is recorded of John's baptism, that they "went out unto him, Jerusalem, and all Judea, and all the regions round about the Jordan; and they were baptized of him in the river Jordan, confessing their sins." (Matt. 3:5, 6, cf. Acts 8:36).

4. Going down into the water. The Bible teaches that people not only went to the water but they went down into it. In Acts 8:38 it says concerning Philip and the Eunuch, "And they both went down into the water, both Philip and the Eunuch; and he baptized him." This was an act requiring both the person being baptized and the person doing the baptizing to be in the water.

5. Coming up out of the water. Mark states that after Jesus was baptized, when He was "coming up out of the water, he saw the heavens rent asunder, and the Spirit as a dove descending upon him" (Mark 1:10). Luke writes, in Acts 8:39 "And when they (Philip and the Eunuch) came up out of the water, the Spirit of the Lord caught away Philip; and the Eunuch saw him no more, for he went on his way rejoicing."

From the New Testament one would conclude that baptism was an act that took much water, the candidate went to the water, went down into it, along with the administrator and then came up out of it. All these requirements would be useless if the act of baptism required only a few drops of water placed on the candidate's head. The act of immersion, however, requires all these conditions. The Scriptures then definitely point toward immersion in water as being New Testament baptism.

B. *The symbolism of baptism.* Since man lives in a physical world, God has given physical acts or ordinances to teach him spiritual truth. This is true of baptism. Baptism is not just a physical act. It is an act filled with spiritual meaning.

1. Baptism is a picture of a burial and a resurrection. In Romans 6:1-5, we read of this great spiritual meaning.

Baptism is actually a drama which portrays two significant acts. Paul says "all we who were baptized into Christ Jesus were baptized into His death? We were buried therefore with Him through Baptism into death: that like as Christ was raised from the dead through the glory of the Father, so we also might walk in newness of life." (Romans 6:3, 4). The death, burial, and resurrection of Christ for the sins of man is the greatest event in all history. God desired that man should never forget this, therefore he gave the act of baptism. Whenever one sees the act of baptism, he should see first of all Christ dying on the cross, being buried in Joseph's tomb, and being raised again on the third day. This reminds the Christian contantly that Jesus loved him and gave His life for him.

A second picture that one sees in baptism is that of the individual who has died to sin through faith and repentance, being now buried in the watery grave of baptism. The old man of sin having been crucified, is now buried and separated from the penitent believer. Baptism is the burial ceremony for the old man of sin—this person is baptized into Christ, he is joined to Him, united with Him, then, he is raised a new man in Christ, to walk in a "newness" or new way of life.

No action, except immersion, carries all this rich symbolic meaning. Baptism is intended to glorify Christ by constantly reminding us of His sacrifice and resurrection. To change baptism from immersion, not only departs from the plain teaching of the scripture but robs Christ of the honor which is due Him.

Professor J. W. McGarvey, writing concerning this, said:

> When I was in Palestine, if I could have found beyond all doubt the very sepulchre of Joseph, in which the Saviour was laid away, where he lay so still until the resurrection morning, I would have prized the sight of it above all that I saw. I would have been glad to go in and to stretch myself on the same bare rock floor, to have some friend roll

LESSONS IN CHRISTIAN DOCTRINE

a stone to the mouth of it, that I might realize by imagination my Saviour's burial. We can not do that; we are not permitted to do it; but in this ordinance of baptism we are allowed to do the next thing to it. Laid down in a watery grave in obedience to His command, we allow the water to close above our heads, and then, as though we were dead, we are lifted by the strong arm of the servant of God out of that cold grave and we start to walk in a new life as He started to walk in a new one when he arose from the dead. (Cowden—Christian Worship, pp. 220-21)

2. Baptism, a picture of a birth. Jesus, in John 3:5, told Nicodemus, "Except one be born of water and the Spirit, he can not enter into the kingdom of God." The scriptures teach that a Christian is a new creature. "Wherefore if any man is in Christ, he is a new creature: the old things are passed away; behold, they are become new." (II Cor. 5:17). The act of Baptism graphically conveys this meaning. Paul refers to baptism as the "washing of regeneration," or "cleansing (bath) of the new birth" (Titus 3:5, Amplified).

The Christian is begotten or conceived by the Spirit through the Word of God, and is born of water. In the act of immersion this picture of a birth is quite clear.

C. *The meaning of the Greek word.* The Greek language, which is the original language of the New Testament, was very precise and accurate. A word was seldom used to convey more than one meaning. This is true in the case of the word that is translated baptism. The Greek is "baptizo". It means "to dip, immerse or plunge." This is not denied by any serious student of the word.

If Jesus had wanted to say pour, He would have used the word "ekcheo." It meant to "pour out." Had Jesus desired to say sprinkle, He would have used the word "rantizo," which means "to sprinkle." It is evident that Jesus meant to command immersion because without exception He and the Apostles used the word "baptizo," which means "immerse."

From our study we have found that the plain statements of scripture, regarding the act of baptism, the symbolism embodied in the act and the Greek word, which Christ used, all indicate that baptism is an immersion in water.

III. THE PERSON TO BE BAPTIZED

The next question to be considered is, who is the proper subject for baptism? What kind of person is to be baptized? Not every person is ready to be baptized. There are certain pre-requisites to the act of baptism.

60

BAPTISM

A. *A Person must be a believer in Christ.* Jesus said, "He that believeth and is baptized shall be saved." (Mark 16:16). In Acts 18:8 we read, "And many of the Corinthians hearing believed, and were baptized." There is no commandment to baptize those who are too young to believe or who are not capable of believing. The Scripture further teaches that those to be baptized must be teachable. In the Great Commission, Jesus said, "Go ye therefore and teach all nations, baptizing them. . . ." (Matt. 28:19). The New Testament teaches that a person must be a believer in Christ before he can be baptized.

B. *A person is not only to be a believer but he should be a penitent believer.* Repentance is also required before baptism. Peter told the 3,000 on Pentecost, who through faith asked him what they must do to be saved, "Repent ye and be baptized everyone of you in the name of Jesus Christ unto the remission of your sins. . . ." (Acts 2:38). The one who has not sinned has nothing of which to repent and is therefore not to be baptized. Neither is one who has sinned and will not repent a proper subject for baptism. Romans 6 teaches that baptism is a burial in water of one who has died to sin. It is evident that before one can be scripturally baptized, he must have, through faith in Christ, and repentance from sin, died to sin, before he is to be buried with his Lord in baptism. The candidate for baptism must have repented of his sins.

C. *Though not specifically commanded, there seems to have been a public confession of Christ preceding baptism in the New Testament.* This is indicated in the case of the Eunuch in Acts 8:37. Paul seems to imuly this in Romans 10:10 when he says, "For with the heart man believeth unto righteousness; and with the mouth confession is made unto salvation."

The New Testament teaches that the person to be baptized is to be a penitent believer in Christ as the Son of God.

IV. THE PROPER PURPOSE FOR BAPTISM

The next logical question is, why should one be baptized? Of what value is it to the believer? In order to answer this, we need to find out what purpose Jesus gave to it. Different religious groups teach widely varying opinions regarding the purpose of baptism. One group says that baptism has nothing to do with a person's salvation. After he is saved he is baptized because he is saved. They teach that it is utter irony to baptize a person in order that he may be saved—in other words, before he is saved. Another group teaches that

61

baptism alone, if administered by the proper person, will save an individual.

It is evident that both views can not be correct. It is possible that neither are. Christ gave the commandment for baptism. He alone is qualified to state the purpose.

Jesus and the Apostles commanded baptism for these reasons:

A. *In order to be saved.* Mark 16:16, "He that believeth and is baptized shall be saved; but he that disbelieveth shall be condemned." Jesus says that one is to be baptized in order to be saved. Peter repeats this thought when he tells how Noah and his family were saved during the flood by water. He continues, "The like figure whereunto even baptism *doth also now save us* (not the putting away of the filth of the flesh, but the answer of a good conscience toward God,) by the resurrection of Jesus Christ" (I Peter 3:21, KJ).

B. *For the remission of sins.* When the 3,000 on Pentecost asked what they should do to be saved, Peter seeing their faith in Christ replied, ". . . Repent ye, and be baptized every one of you in the name of Jesus Christ unto the remission of your sins; and ye shall receive the gift of the Holy Spirit."

Peter was an Apostle. A few hours before this Christ had sent from heaven the Holy Spirit to guide him. When he gave the above instructions, he was speaking as an inspired Apostle and as God's spokesman, revealing to man God's requirements for salvation.

Jesus had also told Peter that He would give to him the keys of the Kingdom of Heaven; "And whatsoever thou shalt bind on earth shall be bound in heaven; and whatsoever thou shalt loose on earth shal lbe loosed in heaven" (Matt. 16:19). Peter's statement in Acts 2:38 came directly from the throne of God. When Peter said that baptism, coupled with faith and repentance, would obtain the remission of sins, one can not—dare not—doubt it!

C. *For washing away of sin.* When Jesus appeared to Paul on the road to Damascus, He did not tell him what to do to be saved. When Paul asked what he should do, Jesus replied, "Arise, and go into Damascus; and there it shall be told thee of all things which are appointed for thee to do" (Acts 22:10). When Ananias came he said to Saul "And now why tarriest thou? arise, and be baptized, and wash away thy sins, calling on his name" (Acts 22:16). Paul believed in Jesus when he saw Him on the road. He had spent three days in penitent prayer and yet his sins were still with him. Ananias told him that he lacked one thing. That was baptism. Baptism

BAPTISM

alone will not take away sin, but Jesus and the Apostles clearly state that when it is preceded by faith in Christ and repentance of sin, that it does procure for the penitent believer God's forgiveness.

D. *Baptism into Christ.* Paul told the Romans, "Know ye not, that so many of us as were *baptized into Jesus Christ* were baptized into his death?" (Romans 6:3, KJ). He told the Galatians, "For ye are all the children of God by faith in Christ Jesus. For as many of you as have been *baptized into Christ* have put on Christ." (Galatians 3:26, 37, KJ). Baptism then is *into* Christ.

This is a meaningful statement. The New Testament teaches that redemption is *in Christ*, (Romans 3:24); there is no condemnation *in Christ*, (Romans 8:1); there is consolation *in Christ* (Phil. 2:1). The Bible also teaches that all will be made alive in the resurrection morning *in Christ*, (I Cor. 15:22) and that if any man is *in Christ*, he is a new creature (II Cor. 5:17). All these blessings are promised to those *in Christ.* The New Testament states that in order to get into *Christ*, that we must be baptized into Him. One can not be saved outside of Him!

It is clear that salvation comes *after*, not before the act of baptism. It is also clear that baptism alone will not save a person. But the New Testament teaches that when a person who trully believes in Christ and genuinely repents of sin, he is then to be baptized into Christ for the remission of his sins.

Professor F. F. Bruce states, "The idea of an unbaptized Christian is simply not entertained in the New Testament."

QUESTIONS — BAPTISM

MATCHING:

_____ 1. "Repent, and be baptized every one of you in the name of Jesus Christ for the remission of sins."

_____ 2. "And Jesus, when he was baptized, went up straightway out of the water."

_____ 3. "He that believeth and is baptized shall be saved."

_____ 4. "Buried with him in baptism."

_____ 5. "The like figure whereunto even baptism doth also now save us."

63

_____ 6. "And when they were come up out of the water, the Spirit of the Lord caught away Philip."

_____ 7. "And many of the Corinthians hearing believed, and were baptized."

_____ 8. "Arise, and be baptized, and wash away thy sins."

_____ 9. "Go ye therefore, and teach all nations, baptizing them . . ."

a. I Pet. 3:21   d. Mark 16:16   g. Acts 22:16
b. Rom. 6:4   e. Acts 18:8   h. Acts 2:38
c. Acts 8:39   f. Matt. 3:16   i. Matt. 28:19

COMPLETE:

1. Baptism is a symbol or picture of what? _____

_____

2. Why is an infant not a proper subject for baptism?_____

_____

_____

3. List four (4) blessings promised to those in Christ.

a. _____

b. _____

c. _____

d. _____

Lesson Eight

THE LORD'S SUPPER

I. The Lord's Supper given.
   A. The occasion.
   B. The elements used.
      1. The bread.
      2. The fruit of the vine.

II. The names.
   A. Breaking of Bread.
   B. Table of the Lord.
   C. The Lord's Supper.
   D. The Communion.

III. When to partake.
   A. Plain Scriptural examples.
      1. Stated meeting.
      2. Stated purpose.
   B. Weekly communion taught by implication.
   C. Argument from type.
   D. Testimonies of the Church Fathers.

IV. The Significance of the Lord's Supper.
   A. A memorial of Christ's death.
   B. A proclamation.

In our nation's Capital, the Washington Monument reaches high into the sky, in memory of the first President of the United States. In the same city, the Lincoln Memorial stands in honor of another great President. A few miles away in Virginia is the tomb of the Unknown Soldier, built in Arlington Cemetery. It is placed there in memory of those unknown military men who gave their lives in their country's service. These are the ways that man erects monuments so that those who pass by may call to mind the one in whose honor it was built.

All such memorials eventually crumble or decay. When Jesus Christ determined to leave a monument to His name, He gave one that would stand as long as the earth remains. That memorial is the Lord's Supper.

When man builds memorials, he likes to secure rare and expensive metals and stones. Jesus, in choosing the elements for His memorial, chose very common materials: bread and grape juice. Wheat and grapes will grow in almost every part of the world. Jesus' memorial can be observed around the world.

Man builds his memorials out of the most durable materials he can find. Christ, on the other hand, chose very fragile and perishable materials. Bread will quickly mold and dry up. Grape juice, left for a short time, will sour and spoil. This indicates that Jesus did not expect His monument to last because of the substance of which it was made. Rather He knew that the permanence of His memorial would depend on the love of God in the hearts of His people.

I. THE LORD'S SUPPER GIVEN

A. *The Occasion.* The occasion that Jesus chose to institute the Lord's Supper was the annual Passover Feast of the Jews. Since it was the last Passover before Jesus' death, He especially wanted to eat this feast with His apostles. (Luke 22:15, 16). During the Passover meal, there were four cups of wine which they drank ceremonially. Following one of these, presumably the third cup, (cf. Luke 22:17 and I Cor. 10:16) was the time Jesus chose to give the Lord's Supper.

Compared to the elaborate Passover Feast, the new institution was very simple. Jesus took bread and gave thanks; broke it and gave to the Apostles saying, "this is my body which is given for you: this do in remembrance of me" (Luke 22:19). When they had eaten the bread, Jesus took a cup containing the fruit of the vine, gave thanks, and gave it to them saying, "Drink ye all of it; for this is my blood of the covenant which is shed for many unto remission of sins" (Matt. 26:27, 28).

B. *The elements used.*

1. The bread. The bread which Jesus used in the Lord's Supper was presumably the unleavened bread of the Passover Feast. The day before the Passover began, every Jewish family would dispose of all leaven in their homes. For seven days

they would eat only unleavened bread. (Deut. 16:3, 4). This was to remind them of their hasty departure from Egypt (Exodus 12:39). There is no indication that Jesus brought any other bread with Him. The concept that leaven represents evil is another point of evidence in favor of unleavened bread. (cf. I Cor. 5:6-8).

2. The fruit of the vine. The second part of the Lord's Supper is referred to as the "cup" or "fruit of the vine." (Mk. 14:23, 25; Matt. 26:27, 29). The term fruit of the vine refers to grape juice. God had referred to grape juice as the "blood of the grape" (Deut. 32:14). It is significant that Jesus chose the "blood of the grape" to picture the "blood of the covenant," our Saviour's blood.

Whether the cup contained fermented or unfermented grape juice is a debated question. Some authorities maintain that it was fermented, arguing that the Jews could not have kept the grape juice sweet since the fall harvest. Others contend that it could have been unfermented since the ancients did have ways of keeping it unfermented for as long as a year. Since Jesus did not specify either fermented or unfermented grape juice, the church is not bound to either. Today with the many ways of preserving, unfermented juice certainly is more fitting and in keeping with the total meaning of the Lord's Supper.[1]

II. THE NAMES

A. *Breaking of Bread.* The most frequently used term in the New Testament for this Christian Feast is the Breaking of Bread. In Acts 20:7 it speaks of the disciples coming together on the first day of the week "to Break Bread." Acts 2:42 states that the early Church "continued stedfastly in the Apostles teaching and fellowship and in the *Breaking of Bread* and the prayers." This expression is also used in I Corinthians 10:16. This description of the Lord's Supper seems to be taken from the action of the Lord the night He gave it. Matthew, Mark, and Luke, as well as the Apostle Paul, in I Corinthians 11, record that Jesus took the bread, gave thanks for it and broke it saying, "Take eat, this is My body." The following day when the body of Jesus was cut and pierced, the Apostles received a graphic picture of what Christ meant. How sacred was the hour when the disciples would "break" the loaf in memory of the Lord's broken body!

B. *Table of the Lord.* Paul reminds the Corinthians "Ye can not partake of the Table of the Lord, and of the table of

---

1. For a good discussion of the pros and cons of this question read: *Christian Standard,* "The Lord's Supper", by James Van Buren, May 3, 1953; *Christian Standard,* "The Beverage of Grape Juice", by Donald Nash, June 13, 1953.

demons" (I Cor. 10:21 ASV). This name reminds us that the Table belongs to Christ. He gave it in the first place, He is also the host at every meal. Jesus gave His Apostles the precious promise that "where two or three are gathered together in my name, there am I in the midst of them" (Matt. 18:20). This is true at all gatherings of the Church. It is significantly so when the Table is spread.

This sublime truth needs emphasizing today. One church, in order to stress this thought, did this. They moved the Communion table out from the pulpit, far enough to place a chair between the table and the pulpit. The Elders sat at each end but the chair behind the table was always vacant. This was a silent reminder that Christ, the host, was present at the meal.

C. *The Lord's Supper.* The Lord's Supper is perhaps the most familiar term used today. It is called the *Lord's Supper* because He is the one who gave it. He invites His children to come and eat. He is the one rejected when a Christian fails to be present at this meal. As one partakes, it is Christ who is the source of spiritual food. It is Christ who invites "this do in remembrance of me" (Luke 22:19). It is also Christ alone who can debar a child of God from this Table. It is truly the *Lord's Supper.*

The name Supper was no doubt given because it was at an evening meal that Jesus gave it. The one clear example of its observance in the New Testament was in the evening (Acts 20:7).

D. *The Communion.* The term "Communion" is often applied today to the Lord's Supper. The use of the word "Communion" in the New Testament seems to be more of a description of what takes place, than a name for it. Paul reminds the Corinthians "The cup of blessings which we bless, is it not a communion of the blood of Christ? The bread which we break, is it not a communion of the body of Christ?" (I Cor. 10:16). The word Communion means to share, or participate in. Paul is saying that when we drink the cup or eat the bread, that we share or participate in the blessings and benefits of the Lord's death on the cross. We also share the meal with Christ as our host. It is a communion or sharing in the finest sense of the word.

III. WHEN TO PARTAKE

When Jesus gave the Lord's Supper He did not specify the time or frequency of observance. Jesus left many things for the Holy Spirit to teach the Apostles (John 16:12-13). He simply said do this in memory of Me. When the Church was established on Pentecost, the Apostles were careful to follow

THE LORD'S SUPPER

His admonition. Luke states that the church "continued steadfastly in the Apostles teaching and fellowship, in *the breaking of bread* and the prayers" (Acts 2:42). The word steadfastly indicates that they did this continuously, devoting themselves constantly to the worship of God. Some think that they may have observed the Lord's Supper daily for a while. In Acts 2:46, we read "And day by day, continuing steadfastly with one accord in the temple, and *breaking bread at home,* they took their food with gladness and singleness of heart." Since Luke mentions the partaking of food in the last clause, the expression "breaking bread" may be the Lord's Supper.

The first clear evidence as to the frequency of its observance is found in Acts 20:7. "And upon the first day of the week, when the disciples came together to break bread, Paul preached unto them, ready to depart on the morrow; and continued his speech until midnight." As proof that weekly communion was the practice of the early church, we present the following arguments.

A. *Plain Scriptural examples.* All the facts concerning this meeting in Troas go to prove that it was a stated meeting for a stated purpose.

1. Stated meeting. The use of the definite article "the" implies that the Christians at Troas were accustomed to meeting on the first day of every week. Paul arrived from Philippi on Monday, prior to this meeting, because Luke states that he tarried in Troas seven days. Paul was hurrying toward Jerusalem that he might be there for Pentecost (Acts 20:16). This is further shown by the fact that Paul left early Monday morning following his meeting with the Church. To meet with the church on the first day of the week Paul had tarried seven days. This would indicate that worship on the first day of the week was an established custom in Troas. If this were true in Troas, it was surely true in the other churches that had been established under the direction of the Apostles.

2. Stated purpose. Luke clearly states that they met for the purpose of breaking bread. "And upon the first day of the week, when the disciples came *together to break bread,* Paul preached unto them, ready to depart on the morrow; and continued his speech until midnight" (Acts 20:7). The church did not come together to hear Paul preach. They were accustomed to meeting regularly to break bread. Since Paul was in town that day I am sure they gladly heard him speak, but this was not the primary purpose for their gathering. Those who use this passage to prove weekly worship, but deny weekly communion, involve themselves in a contradiction. This Scripture does give an example of weekly worship, but at the same time it establishes the Apostolic example of the weekly break-

69

ing of the bread. Any effort to disprove one, will at the same time disprove both.

B. *Weekly communion taught by implication.* In I Corinthians 11, Paul gives instructions to correct the abuses surrounding the Lord's Table at Corinth. He chastises them for their abuse of the Lord's Table in these words, "when therefore ye assemble yourselves together, it is not possible to eat the Lord's Supper" (I Cor. 11:20, ASV). Their conduct about the Table prevented them from truly eating the Supper in an acceptable manner. This Scripture would imply that their conduct prevented them from carrying out the main purpose for which they came together, that of eating the Lord's Supper. If someone were to say that when the ball team arrived on the field they were not able to play ball because of the rain, anyone would understand that the purpose for the coming was to play ball. This same truth is obvious in I Corinthians 11:20.

This also agrees with our proposition, since the church at Corinth did practice weekly worship. This is found in I Corinthians 16:2. The Scriptures would imply that as often as the church at Corinth met together, which was weekly, they observed the Lord's Supper.

C. *Argument from type.* When God gave Moses the blueprint for the Tabernacle, He was doing more than merely giving him a tent in which to worship during the wilderness travels. The Tabernacle was a teaching instrument to prepare Israel for the coming of Christ. It is generally thought that the Tabernacle court was a picture of the world; the Holy Place, was a type of the church today and that the Holy of Holies depicted Heaven.

In the Holy Place, which represented the church today, there were three pieces of furniture.

The Golden Lampstand which furnished light for the room, was a picture of God's word. The Word gives light and guidance to the pathway of man (Psalm 119:105; 119:130).

The Golden Altar upon which incense was burned, fittingly represents the prayers of the Saints of God as they are lifted to the heavenly throne (Rev. 5:8).

The other piece of furniture was the Table of Shewbread. Each week the priests were commanded to place twelve loaves of shewbread on it. They remained on the Table for one week. New loaves would then be placed on the Table and the priests would eat the old loaves in worship of Jehovah. The word "shewbread" literally means, "presence bread." To Israel this reminded them of God's presence and blessings and providential care. This certainly would find fulfillment in the Lord's Supper today. The loaf and the cup vividly remind the Christian that Christ is with us and that through Him we receive all blessings from God. The fact that the priests faithfully ate once a week, would lend support to the teaching of weekly communion.

D. *Testimonies of the Church Fathers.* The term Church Fathers or Apostolic Fathers refers to the leaders in the Church immediately following the Apostles. The writings of these men are not considered inspired but they do present a picture of the Church and its worship, as it was conducted immediately after the days of the Apostles.

One of these men was Justin Martyr. He wrote about 150 A.D. He was a disciple of Polycarp who had been a disciple of the Apostle John. Being that close to the Apostle John, one could expect his teachings to be in accordance with the Apostles. He gives an account of the worship of the Church in his day as follows:

> And on the day called Sunday, all who live in cities or in the country gather together to one place, and the memoirs of the Apostles or the writings of the prophets are read, as long as time permits; then when the reader has ceased, the president verbally instructs, and exhorts to the imitation of these good things. Then we all rise together and pray, and, as we before said, when our prayer is ended, bread and wine and water are brought, and the president in like manner offers prayers and thanksgivings, according to his ability, and the people assent, saying Amen; and there is a distribution to each, and a participation of that over which thanks have been given, and to those who are absent a portion is sent by the deacons.[1]

Other church fathers could be quoted but this will suffice. It is evident that the early church did eat the Lord's Supper weekly and continued this practice for two centuries.

Robert Milligan says, "During the first two centuries the practice of weekly communion was universal, and it was continued in the Greek Church till the seventh century. Such as neglected it three weeks in succession were excommunicated" (Milligan's Scheme of Redemption, Page 440).

IV. THE SIGNIFICANCE OF THE LORD'S SUPPER

A. *A memorial of Christ's death.* The Lord's Supper is a weekly Table of Remembrance. A memorial should serve at least three functions. These are admirably done in the Lord's Supper.

---

1. Moxe, A. Cleveland, *The Apostolic Fathers with Justin Martyr and Irenaeus.* "Weekly Worship of the Christians.", Chapter LXII., Page 185-6.

1. It satisfies the desire of the heart to do some tender, loving thing for the Master. The Lord's Supper provides this opportunity. Jesus had this in mind when He said, "This *do* in remembrance of me" (I Cor. 11:24).

2. By frequent observance, it does not permit us to forget, but like a time piece of the soul, summons the believer to the foot of the cross.

3. By its symbolic import, it constantly reminds of the very significant fact of Christianity which is "that Christ died for our sins according to the Scriptures" (I Cor. 15:3).

Alexander Campbell speaks effectively of the memorial facet of the Lord's Supper when he says: "Upon the loaf and upon the cup of the Lord, in letters which speak not to the eye, but to the heart of every disciple, is inscribed, 'When this you see, remember Me.' Indeed, the Lord says to each disciple, when he receives the symbols into his hand, 'This is My body broken for you. This is My blood shed for you'" (The Christian System, 1835, pp. 265-291).

B. *A proclamation.* Each Lord's Day, as the disciple sits at the table with his Lord, he is preaching a sermon.

1. First of all Paul says that when we eat we proclaim the Lord's death (I Cor. 11:26). Jesus said when He gave the Lord's Supper "This cup is the New Covenant in My blood" (Luke 22:20). The Lord's Supper is a monument to our salvation as well as to Christ Himself. The Lord's Supper proclaims that man is redeemed and receives forgiveness of sins through the blood of Christ (Ephesians 1:7; I Peter 1:18-20).

2. Secondly, we proclaim our love for Him. When the Christian assembles at the Table, he is telling the Lord and the world that he believes that the blood of Christ redeems and that he is there to show his love to Christ by being obedient to His command. The love of Christ that caused Him to die for man when he was weak and helpless (Romans 5:6-8) is the love that brings the Christian to love Christ and to be present at His table.

3. We proclaim the Lord's return. Paul states that when we partake of the Lord's Supper, we "proclaim the Lord's death till He comes" (I Cor. 11:26). The Lord's Table looks back in memory to Calvary where our salvation was made possible. It also looks forward to the day when Christ shall return and our salvation will be fully realized. This is the grand consummation of the scheme of redemption, when the redeemed of all ages will be gathered to be with their Lord who has redeemed them from sin. Only those who truly anticipate His second coming will consistently participate in this Supper.

THE LORD'S SUPPER

QUESTIONS — THE LORD'S SUPPER

Read the four accounts of the institution of the Lord's Supper—Matthew 26:26-29; Mark 14:22-25; Luke 22:19-20; I Corinthians 11:23-25. In the blanks write the reference where the following statement is found:

_____ 1. "And he took bread, and gave thanks, and brake it, and gave unto them."

_____ 2. "Take, eat: this is my body, which is broken for you; this do in remembrance of me."

_____ 3. "And he took the cup, and when he had given thanks, he gave it to them."

_____ 4. "And they all drank of it."

_____ 5. "For this is my blood of the new testament, which is shed for many for the remission of sins."

_____ 6. "I will not drink henceforth of this fruit of the vine, until that day when I drink it new with you in my Father's kingdom."

DISCUSS:

1. List three (3) names applied to the Lord's Supper.

   a. _____.

   b. _____.

   c. _____.

2. List the four (4) arguments in favor of weekly communion.

   a. _____.

   b. _____.

   c. _____.

   d. _____.

3. In what sense is the Lord's Supper a proclamation.

   _____

   _____

   _____

73

Lesson Nine

PRAYER

I. Beginning of Prayer.

II. What is Prayer?
   A. Petitions or Supplications.
   B. Thanksgiving and Praise.

III. Conditions for effective prayer.
   A. Pray with pure hearts and clean hands.
   B. We must hear and do God's will.
   C. Pray humbly in harmony with God's will.
   D. Pray fervently and with persistence.
   E. Prayers must be unselfish.
   F. In the name of Christ.
   G. Pray in faith.
   H. Pray with a forgiving spirit.
   I. Without pretension or vain repetition.

IV. The Holy Spirit's assistance in prayer.

V. God has promised answers to prayer.

I. BEGINNING OF PRAYER

The first mention of prayer in the Bible is in Genesis 4:26, "Then began men to call upon the name of Jehovah." There is no mention of God commanding men to pray. Prayer seems to have begun freely and spontaneously. Man felt his need for God and began to call upon Him. Prayer to God should be as natural an action as a child talking to its Father and Mother. When man truly knows and understands God, he will desire to talk to Him.

PRAYER

II. WHAT IS PRAYER?

A. *Petitions or Supplications.* Supplication — earnestly seeking God's blessings — is at the very heart of prayer. Prayer always springs out of a sense of need, either oneself (petition) or for others (intercession). This sense of need is joined with a belief that God is a rewarder of them that diligently seek Him. (Hebrew 11:6.)

Jesus urged his disciples to ". . . ask and it shall be given you; seek, and ye shall find; knock, and it shall be opened unto you" (Matt. 7:7). Even though God knows our needs before we ask, He still is glad to have His children come to Him with their desires. He finds a joy in providing those things which are essential to our life and wellbeing here on earth.

B. *Thanksgiving and Praise.* A second important part of prayer is thanksgiving and praise. As petitions indicate one's needs, praise and thanksgiving reflect one's grateful attitude toward God. Paul instructed the Philippians not to be anxious "but in everything by prayer and supplication, *with thanksgiving* let your requests be made known unto God" (Phil. 4:6). Paul writes to Timothy "I exhort therefore, first of all, that supplications, prayers, intercessions, thanksgiving be made for all men" (I Timothy 2:1).

Thanksgiving and praise to God demonstrate gratitude on the part of man for former blessings received from God. This unquestionably is pleasing to God; it is due Him and will no doubt help assure the answer to our petitions. The Thessalonian brethren were told "in everything give thanks: for this is the will of God in Christ Jesus to you ward" (I Thessalonians 5:18).

III. CONDITIONS FOR EFFECTIVE PRAYER

God's promises are always conditional. This principle holds true with prayer. He has promised to answer our prayers. But He has also laid down certain conditions which man must meet, before God will answer his prayers. Here are a few of those conditions.

A. *Pray with pure hearts and clean hands.* "If I regard iniquity in my heart, The Lord will not hear" (Psalm 66:18, ASV). "I desire therefore that the men play in every place, lifting up holy hands, without wrath and disputing" (I Timothy 2:8, (ASV).

God is a holy God. There is no sin in Him and He will not tolerate sin in those who come into His presence through prayer. These Scriptures refer to sin in the lives of His chil-

75

dren. When He says He will not hear He is speaking of hearing favorably their requests. This does not refer to prayer for forgiveness; prayer out of a heart of repentance. God has promised to answer that prayer (I John 1:9; cf. Acts 8:22). He is here speaking of a Christian asking for some blessing while refusing to repent of sin in his life. God does not hear and answer that prayer.

God told Israel, "Behold, Jehovah's hand is not shortened, that it cannot save; neither his ear heavy, that it cannot hear: but your iniquities have separated between you and your God and your sins have hid his face from you, so that he will not hear" (Isaiah 59:1-2). One of the best guarantees that God will hear our prayers is to begin them with a sincere request for forgiveness. This is always pleasing to Him.

B. *We must hear and do God's will.* John reminds us, "whatsoever we ask we receive of him, because we keep his commandments and do the things that are pleasing in his sight" (I John 3:22). A second condition for effective prayer is to keep God's commandments. Proverbs 28:9 states, "He that turneth away his ear from hearing the law, Even his prayer is an abomination" (ASV). God is not foolish. He will not continue to pour His blessings on a willful and disobedient child. Nothing pleases a parent more than to give to a child that is obedient. God feels the same way. One should make sure that he is honestly trying to do the will of the Father before he asks for His blessings and benefits. The blind man stated this thought aptly when he said in John 9:31, "We know that God heareth not sinners: but if any man be a worshipper of God, and doeth His will, him He heareth."

C. *Pray humbly in harmony with God's will.* Jesus illustrated this principle when in the Garden of Gethsemane He prayed earnestly, "O my Father, if it be possible, let this cup pass from Me: nevertheless, not as I will, but as thou wilt" (Matt. 26:39). The Father's will must always be first in our prayers. John says, "And this is the boldness which we have toward him, that, if we ask anything according to his will, he heareth us" (I John 5:14).

Our heavenly Father who is all wise knows what is best for His kingdom and what is best for us. The Apostle Paul admitted, "we know not how to pray as we ought" (Rom. 8:26). We do not always know what is the Father's will. Therefore, we should ask with the thought that if this is in harmony with His will, and best for His kingdom, we would like to have these blessings. Another reason we should pray that His will be done is because man does not always know what is best for him. Like a child, he may ask for a butcher knife, thinking that this is what he should have. Fortunately, like a wise parent,

PRAYER

God does not always give us what we request. In prayer, we should come to God humbly realizing our lack of knowledge and understanding and leave it to God to decide what blessings we need or do not need.

D. *Pray fervently and with persistence.* James reminds us that "The effectual fervent prayer of a righteous man availeth much" (James 5:16b). The earnest supplication of a righteous man is very powerful. James illustrates this point in verse 17 by reminding us of Elijah's fervent prayer that it would not rain. God withheld rain for three years and six months. Again Elijah prayed and God sent the rain. An earnest prayer, God hears. Undoubtedly, an apathetic, half-hearted prayer is detestable to God. It reflects the insincerity and lack of concern on the part of the one praying. A sincere prayer, however, pleases God.

Along with earnestness one must have persistence in prayer also. I Thessalonians 5:17 says "pray without ceasing." This means to pray constantly. Paul tells the Ephesians "Praying at all seasons in the Spirit, and watching thereunto in all perseverance and supplication for all the saints," (Ephesians 6:19). Jesus said, "men ought always to pray, and not to faint" (Luke 18:1).

A number of ministers had gathered to discuss difficult questions, and it was asked how the command to 'pray without ceasing' could be obeyed (I Thessalonians 5:17).

Various suggestions were offered, and at last one of the number was appointed to write an essay on the subject, to be read at the next meeting. A servant who was cleaning heard the discussion and exclaimed,

'What! a whole month to tell the meaning of that text? Why, it's one of the easiest and best verses in the Bible.'

'Well, well, Mary,' said an old minister, 'What do you know about it? Can you pray all the time?'

'Oh, yes sir!'

'What! when you have so many things to do?'

'Why, sir, the more I have to do, the more I can pray.'

'Indeed! well, Mary, how do you do it? Most people wouldn't agree with you.'

'Well, sir,' said the girl, 'when I first open my eyes in the morning, I pray: 'Lord, open the eyes of my understanding'; and while I am dressing, I pray that I may be clothed with the robe of righteousness;

while I am washing, I ask to have my sins washed away. As I begin work, I pray that I may have strength for all the work of the day; while I kindle the fire, I pray that revival may be kindled in me. While preparing and eating breakfast, I ask to be fed with the Bread of Life and the pure milk of the Word. As I sweep the house, I pray that my heart may be swept clean of all its impurities. And as I am busy with the little children, I look up to God as my Father and pray that I may always have the trusting love of a little child—and so on all day. Everything I do gives me a thought for prayer . . .'

'Enough, enough!' cried the minister, 'these things are often hid from the wise and prudent and revealed unto babes, as the Lord Himself said. Go on, Mary,' he continued, 'pray without ceasing. As for us, let us thank the Lord for this lesson.'[1]

E. *Prayers must be unselfish.* Another condition for effective prayer is that they must be unselfish. James reminded the people of his day, "Ye ask, and receive not, because ye ask amiss, that ye may spend it in your pleasures" (James 4:3, ASV). One should always put God's kingdom and His will first. A request must first be viewed or weighed in the light of God's program. We must ask ourselves "Am I asking for this in order to be a better worker for Christ? Do I need this to forward His kingdom? Will I be a better Christian and will Christ's kingdom be blessed if I receive my petition?" It is so easy to think of God as a glorified Santa Claus to whom we can go for every desire we may have. This image of God is not true. He must keep our spiritual welfare and His kingdom first in mind. Often times, we would be ruined if God answered every selfish request that we made. In His love and wisdom, however, He chooses the things that we need and will help us grow spiritually. This is another reason why we should always pray, "Thy will be done."

F. *Pray in the name of Christ.* Another condition for effective prayer is that in this Christian age prayer is to be directed to the Father in the name of Christ. Jesus told His Apostles, "And whatsoever ye shall ask in my name, that will I do, that the Father may be glorified in the Son. If ye shall ask anything in my name, that will I do," (John 14:13-14). Again He reminds them, "Hitherto have ye asked nothing in my name : ask, and ye shall receive that your joy may be made full" (John 16:24).

1. Tract, *Pray Without Ceasing,* Scottdale, Pennsylvania, Herald Press.

PRAYER

The Apostles had not known to ask in Jesus' name before but now they do. There are a number of reasons why the Christian should pray to God in the name of Christ.

1. Our access to the Father was made possible by the sacrifice of Christ. "Therefore, brethren, since we have confidence to enter the sanctuary by the blood of Jesus, by the new and living way which he opened for us through the curtain, that is, through his flesh . . ." (Hebrews 10:19-20, RSV). Hebrews 9:8 informs us that the way into the Holy Place or God's presence had not yet been opened while the tabernacle was standing or rather before Christ came into the world. Now, however, through His death and resurrection, He opened up this new and direct communication between earth and heaven (cf. Hebrews 9:11-12). Now through Christ, our High Priest, we may enter God's presence through prayer.

2. Jesus is our mediator. Paul tells Timothy, "For there is one God, one mediator also between God and men, himself man, Christ Jesus." (I Tim. 2:5). A mediator is a "go between." Christ is a Jacob's Ladder to the Christian. Through Him, man may reach heaven with his petitions and praise, and through Christ he may receive heaven's blessings from God. Christ is a two-way channel between earth and heaven.

3. Christ is our intercessor at the throne of God. Paul states that Christ "who is at the right hand of God, who also maketh intercession for us" (Romans 8:34). My name would mean nothing at the throne of God if I did not belong to Christ. Christ has been exalted to a position above every creature in the universe except God (Philippians 2:9). Therefore, when I come to God in the name of Christ, I am coming in the greatest name in heaven and earth, except God, the Father. As one of Christ's redeemed ones, I can come boldly to the throne of God through Him (Hebrews 4:14-16).

4. My sins have been washed away in the blood of Christ. It means that I have been cleansed and made worthy by Him to stand in the presence of God (Rev. 1:5; Hebrews 9:14).

Because of these and other reasons, our prayers to God should always be presented in the name of and by the authority of Jesus Christ our High Priest, Mediator, Saviour, and Lord.

G. *Pray in faith.* Jesus told His Apostles "Therefore I tell you, whatever you ask in prayer. believe that you receive it, and you will" (Mark 11:24, RSV). James tells us that a man should "ask in faith, nothing wavering: for he that wavereth is like a wave of the sea driven with the wind and tossed. For let not that man think that he shall receive any thing of the Lord" (James 1:6-7, KJV). Hebrews 11:6 states the unqualified importance of faith when it says, "But without faith it is impossible to please him: for he that cometh to God must believe that he is, and that he is a rewarder of them that diligently seek him" (Hebrews 11:6).

A Christian can pray in faith because he is coming to God who is all powerful and who can answer the prayers of His children. The Christian can pray in faith knowing he is coming to one who loves him and desires to answer his requests. The Christian has every reason then to pray believing that his prayers will be answered.

One word of caution should be offered. The Christian must always keep in mind that God's will and wisdom will direct God's answer. This does not prevent, however, the Christian praying in faith, believing that God will answer his prayer. Even when God in His wisdom says no to our requests, He still has answered it. He has seen that the request was unwise, so He has said no. Yet He has answered it in the sense that He has heard and answered it in the best way for us. Another thought to keep in mind is that we may ask for one thing believing that to be the thing we desire. God in His wisdom, however, may give us something else which may, for the moment, seem to be a rejection of the request. In the end, though, we may see that God has given us what we really needed and desired but not what we had requested. The following poem illustrates this point.

> I asked God for strength, that I might achieve;
> I was made weak, that I might learn humbly to obey.
> I asked for health, that I might do greater things;
> I was given infirmity, that I might do better things.
> I asked for riches that I might be happy;
> I was given poverty that I might be wise.
> I asked for power that I might have the praise of men;
> I was given weakness, that I might feel the mind of
> God.
> I asked for all things that I might enjoy life;
> I was given life that I might enjoy all things.
> I got nothing I asked for but everything I had hoped for.
> Almost despite myself my unspoken prayers were
> answered;
> I am among men most richly blessed![1]

H. *Pray with a forgiving spirit.* Here is a condition that cannot be overlooked. It is a must if our prayers are to be answered. One of the petitions in the Model Prayer was "forgive us our debts as we also have forgiven our debtors" (Matthew 6:12). This states we are to ask God to forgive us in the same way and to the same extent that we forgive our fellow man.

1. Author **Unknown**

PRAYER

Jesus goes ahead to state "For if ye forgive men their trespasses, your heavenly Father will also forgive you. But if ye forgive not men their trespasses, neither will your Father forgive your trespasses" (Matthew 6:14-15).

To pray with an unforgiving heart, is a sure way to close the doors of heaven to our prayers. It is a complete waste of time to pray that way. One must forgive if he is to be forgiven.

I. *Pray without pretension or vain repetition.* There is perhaps no sin that is more detested by God than the sin of hypocrisy or pretension. On no class or group did Jesus pronounce such severe condemnation as on the hypocrites of His day. Who can forget Jesus' discourse in Matthew 23, when in His last appeal to the Pharisees, He scathingly denounced them with the seven-fold "woe unto you, Scribes and Pharisees, Hypocrites!"

An insincere, pretentious prayer is always an abomination to God. Jesus illustrated this in the story of the Pharisee and the Publican in Luke 18:9-14. The humble Publican went away justified before God. The proud Pharisee remained in his hypocritical sins. God is not deceived by oratory or eloquence. He is impressed only by sincerity. Our prayers then must be simple, direct, and sincere.

A sincere prayer uttered in faith eliminates unnecessary, repetitious prayers, Jesus told His Apostles "And in praying use not vain repetitions, as the Gentiles do for they think that they shall be heard for their much speaking" (Matthew 6:7). This does not mean that we should not persist in prayer nor that we may not at times pray at great length. Jesus often times would spend a night in prayer, or rise long before dawn to pray (cf. Luke 9:28; Mark 1:35). Jesus does, however, forbid needless repetition of the same thing as though God could not hear or had to be begged to hear His children's prayers.

IV.   THE HOLY SPIRIT'S ASSISTANCE IN PRAYER

One of the great blessings the Christian enjoys is the assistance of the Holy Spirit in prayer. Paul says "And in like manner the Spirit also helpeth our infirmity: for we know not how to pray as we ought; but the Spirit himself maketh intercession for us with groanings which cannot be uttered" (Rom. 8:26). The Christian needs this help in prayer since he does not always know what is best for him or the kingdom. The Christian is limited in prayer because he does not know what tomorrow may bring. Also the Christian does not always know how to express in words exactly the longing and desires of his heart.

81

LESSONS IN CHRISTIAN DOCTRINE

For these and other reasons, our heavenly Father has given us His Holy Spirit to assist us in prayer. He takes our petitions and praise and presents them correctly to the throne of God. He also intercedes for us with God. The Father, the Son, and the Holy Spirit are all involved in prayer. The Christian's prayer is addressed to God the Father, in the name of or by the authority of Christ and with the assistance of the Holy Spirit. Prayer is a wonderful privilege that the Christian enjoys and should always use.

V. GOD HAS PROMISED ANSWERS TO PRAYER

God does answer prayer! This is an attested fact in the scriptures. Moses prayed and his prayer saved a nation from death and from the grave (Exodus 32:14). Joshua prayed, the sun stood still and his enemies were slain by hail stones sent from heaven (Joshua 10:10-14). Hannah prayed and God gave her a son, Samuel (I Samuel 1:9-20).

God's word is filled with the promises of answered prayer.

"For the eyes of the Lord are upon the righteous. And his ears unto their supplication: But the face of the Lord is upon them that do evil" (I Peter 3:12).

"But if any of you lacketh wisdom, let him ask of God, who giveth to all liberally and upbraideth not; and it shall be given him" (James 1:5).

"If ye abide in me, and my words abide in you, ask whatsoever ye will, and it shall be done unto you" (John 15:7; cf. Matt. 7:7; Luke 11:9-10).

If man will meet the conditions that God has laid down for acceptable prayer, he can rest assured that his prayers will be heard and answered according to the will and wisdom of God.

QUESTIONS — PRAYER

TRUE - FALSE

———— 1. Man began to pray when God commanded him to do so.

———— 2. If we ask in faith God will grant our petition whatever it may be.

———— 3. The Holy Spirit assists the Christian to pray correctly.

PRAYER

_____ 4. God does not refuse to hear anyone's prayer.

_____ 5. God may answer prayer and still not give what is requested.

FILL IN THE BLANKS

1. Prayer is composed of two basic parts: _____

   and _____ .

2. List three conditions for effective prayer.

   a. _____ .

   b. _____ .

   c. _____ .

3. List two reasons why the Christian should pray in Christ's name.

   a. _____ .

   b. _____ .

4. Prayer always springs out of a sense of _____ .

   Along with this is a belief that God is a _____ of them that diligently seek Him.

5. Paul says "we know not how to pray as we ought" (Romans 8:26). List three things Christians do not always know.

   a. _____ .

   b. _____ .

   c. _____ .

LESSONS IN CHRISTIAN DOCTRINE

Lesson Ten

GIVING

I. All Things Belong to God.

II. Every Christian is a Steward.

III. Examples of God's Giving.
   A. His Son.
   B. Eternal Life.
   C. Salvation from sin.
   D. Wisdom.

IV. Giving in the Old Testament.
   A. Individual Giving.
      1. The Giving of Cain and Abel.
      2. Noah.
      3. Abraham.
      4. Jacob.
   B. Giving Under the Mosaic Law.
      1. The first tithe commanded.
      2. The second tithe.
      3. The third year tithe.

V. Divine Blessings on the Tithe.

In previous lessons we have discussed how one becomes a Christian and the worship of a Christian through the Lord's Supper and prayer. This chapter continues the worship of the Christian through the act of giving.

84

GIVING

The term "stewardship" covers the various phases of Christian responsibility such as the giving of time and talents, as well as material blessings. This study, however, will confine itself to God's teaching on man's worship through the giving of money. God's word has much to say concerning this. We shall study the basic principles upon which Christian giving rests. Examples of giving, and God's promises to those who do give, will be studied.

The first and perhaps the most basic principle is:

I. ALL THINGS BELONG TO GOD

Moses, in pleading with Israel to obey God, reminded them "Behold, unto Jehovah thy God belongeth heaven and the heaven of heavens, the earth, with all that is therein" (Deut. 10:14). David expressed in poetry the same idea when he said, "The earth is Jehovah's, and the fulness thereof; the world, and they that dwell therein" (Psalm 24:1).

The psalmist emphasized God's ownership of everything, as he wrote "For every beast of the forest is mine, and the cattle upon a thousand hills. I know all the birds of the mountains; and the wild beasts of the field are mine. If I were hungry, I would not tell thee; For the world is mine, and the fulness thereof" (Psalm 50:10-12).

Here are a few of the things that the Bible says belong to God.

a. Silver and gold. "The silver is mine, and the gold is mine, saith Jehovah of hosts" (Haggai 2:8).

b. The rivers. "Because he hath said the river is mine, and I have made it" (Ezekiel 29:9).

c. All land. "And the land shall not be sold in perpetuity; for the land is mine: for ye are strangers and sojourners with me" (Lev. 25:23). God owns the title to all land. He merely grants man the privilege of living on it for a short time. God reminded Israel in Exodus 19:5, "For all the earth is mine."

d. All souls. God told Ezekiel, "Behold, all souls are mine; as the soul of the father, so also the soul of the son is mine . . ." (Ezekiel 18:4).

e. Our bodies. "Or know ye not that your body is a temple of the Holy Spirit which is in you, which ye have from God? and ye are not your own; for ye were bought with a price: glorify God therefore in your body" (I Cor. 6:19-20).

Surely from these scriptures it is clearly seen that "all that is in the heavens and in the earth is thine; thine is the kingdom, O Jehovah, and thou art exalted as head above all" (I Chron. 29:11). The individual who does not recognize God as his owner is said to be more ignorant than the ox or the ass,

85

for Isaiah says, "The ox knoweth his owner, and the ass his master's crib; but Israel doth not know, my people doth no consider" (Isaiah 1:3).

The second principle of Christian giving is that:

II. EVERY CHRISTIAN IS A STEWARD

Jesus gave a parable concerning the talents in Matthew 25:14-30. The servants in the parable represent Christ's disciples. Each man was given a certain number of talents and instructed to use them to the benefit of the king who gave them. Peter writes "As each has received a gift, employ it for one another, as good stewards of God's varied grace" (I Peter 4:10, RSV). A steward is one who oversees and takes care of anothers property. He does not own it, but he administers it on behalf of the owner. Paul tells the Corinthians that the chief qualification for a steward is faithfulness. "Here, moreover, it is required in stewards, that a man be found faithful" (I Cor. 4:2).

Man's relationship to his money and his God becomes clear in the light of these two basic principles: God's ownership of all things and man's stewardship of the things which God gives him. Man owns nothing. Everything he has comes directly or indirectly from God. He is the caretaker of the material blessings which God provides. They are not his to use as he pleases but rather they constitute a trust which he is to handle as God the owner pleases.

Many Christians conceive of their money as belonging to them exclusively, and if they so choose, they may give God some. The reverse, however, is the truth; it all belongs to God and He permits man to use part of it for himself. When this fact is clearly understood it will change the entire attitude of man toward his money and toward his God.

III. EXAMPLES OF GOD'S GIVING

Not only does God own everything, but as Paul says God gives us "richly all things to enjoy" (I Tim. 6:17b). James is very emphatic when he says "every good gift and every perfect gift is from above, coming down from the Father of lights" (James 1:17a). We list just a few of the many blessings which God gives us.

a. His Son. God wrapped His most precious gifts in the person of His Son and sent Him into the world. Jesus says "For God so loved the world, that He *gave* His only begotten Son, that whosoever, believeth on Him should not perish, but have eternal life" (JN. 3:16).

GIVING

b. Eternal life. "For the wages of sin is death; but the free gift of God is *eternal life* in Christ Jesus our Lord" (Romans 6:23). Paul emphasizes that this is a free gift from God. We can not buy it. We can not earn it. We may accept it humbly from God's hands.

c. Salvation from sin. Paul told the Ephesians "For by grace have ye been saved through faith; and that not of yourselves, it is the gift of God" (Eph. 2:8). Again we see that this is a gift from God. This, of course, was made possible through the death of Christ. Peter says, "You know that you were ransomed from the futile ways inherited from your fathers, not with perishable things such as silver or gold, but with the precious blood of Christ, like that of a lamb without blemish or spot" (I Peter 1:18-19, RSV).

d. Wisdom. James says "If any of you lacketh wisdom, let him ask of God, who giveth to all liberally and upbraideth not; and it shall be given him" (James 1:5). We may ask God for many things which in His wisdom He may refuse to give but James assures us that if we will ask for wisdom we shall receive it. This is a gift from God that we should seek constantly.

In addition to all of God's gifts, we know that Christ has also given much to us and for us. John 10:11 states that Christ has given *His life* for His sheep. II Corinthians 8:9 states "For ye know the grace of our Lord Jesus Christ, that, though he was rich, yet for your sakes he became poor, that ye through his poverty might become rich." Christ gave up the riches and glory of heaven that we might obtain those same riches. Truly Paul is correct when he says "Christ loved us and gave himself up for us, a fragrant offering and sacrifice to God" (Ephesians 5:2, RSV).

The poet has well said "the love of God is greater far than tongue or pen can ever tell." He has demonstrated it and continues to as he "giveth to all life, and breath, and all things" (Acts 17:30).

IV. GIVING IN THE OLD TESTAMENT

A. *Individual giving.* Bringing a gift or an offering to God is a practice almost as old as the history of man. Genesis 4 records the first such incident. This giving was done by the sons of Adam and Eve.

1. The giving of Cain and Abel. Genesis does not say that God had commanded Cain and Abel to bring a sacrifice to Him. But Hebrews 11:4 implies this when it says, "by faith Abel offered unto God a more excellent sacrifice than Cain." The

87

statement "by faith" apparently means that God had revealed this to them.

Cain, being a farmer, brought some fruit of the ground as his offering. Abel brought one of the "firstlings of his flock," since he was a shepherd. God accepted Abel's offering but rejected Cain's. Why Cain's offering was rejected is not known for sure. It was evidently rejected because (1) it was the wrong type of offering. Seemingly God desired a blood sacrifice. Or (2) it was an ungenerous gift. Cain may have been too stingy to buy a lamb. This of course caused trouble between the two boys and led to the murder of Abel. However, we see in this incident, the early practice of bringing a gift to God in worship.

2. Noah. When Noah came out of the ark following the flood, the first thing he did was to build an altar unto Jehovah and took of every clean beast and of every clean bird and offered this to God as his offering of thanksgiving and worship for his deliverance. God was pleased with his offering and promised never to smite the earth with a flood.

3. Abraham. By the time of Abraham we find something new in the matter of giving. Abraham still offered animal sacrifices to God, but in addition to this he also gave tithes. In Genesis 14:18-20 is recorded Abraham's encounter with Melchizedek. Abraham had rescued Lot after he had been captured by the four kings. In the capture Abraham had taken considerable spoils. As he returned he met Melchizedek, king of Salem, who was a priest of God Most High. As the priest blessed Abraham, he in turn gave him a tenth of all his goods. Again it is not stated that God had commanded Abraham to do this but in the light of its later practice by Abraham's descendants, it is reasonable to conclude that God had given Abraham the teaching concerning the tithe.

4. Jacob. Abraham's grandson, Jacob, also was a tither. As Jacob left his home on his way to his Uncle Laban's, he spent the night at Bethel. Here he dreamed of the Ladder which stretched from earth to heaven. In the morning, he made a covenant with God, "And Jacob vowed a vow, saying, If God will be with me, and will keep me in this way that I go, and will give me bread to eat, and raiment to put on, so that I come again to my father's house in peace, and Jehovah will be my God, then this stone, which I have set up for a pillar, shall be God's house; and of all that thou shalt give me I will surely give the tenth unto thee" (Gen. 28:20-22). Seemingly God was not offended at Jacob's proposition but rather seemed to be pleased as he continued to bless Jacob both materially and spiritually throughout his life. Apparently Jacob lived up to his vow also.

GIVING

These are examples of giving by individuals during the Patriarchal Age. As we move to the Mosaic period, we will find that God's requirements for giving are much more detailed and demanding.

B. *Giving under the Mosaic Law.* When God gave the law to Moses on Mount Sinai, He made the tithe the primary principle of giving for the Children of Israel. He not only commanded one tithe but seemingly two and possibly three.

1. *The first tithe commanded.* In Leviticus 27 Moses gave the law of tithing. "And all the tithe of the land, whether of the seed of the land, or of the fruit of the tree, is Jehovah's: it is holy unto Jehovah. And if a man will redeem aught of his tithe, he shall add unto it the fifth part thereof. And all the tithe of the herd or the flock, whatsoever passeth under the rod, the tenth shall be holy unto Jehovah. He shall not search whether it be good or bad, neither shall he change it: and if he change it at all, then both it and that for which it is changed shall be holy; it shall not be redeemed" (Lev. 27:30-33). We note these instructions regarding the tithe: (1) They were to give a tenth of all the increase of the land each year. This consisted of the grain which grew on the land, the fruit from the trees or vines. It also included a tithe of the herd and the flock. (2) This was considered to be holy unto Jehovah (Lev. 27:3-32). (3) They seemingly had a specific time when they did this tithing. When it came time to tithe the sheep and the cattle, they would drive them under the rod. A counter would take every tenth sheep or goat or cow and turn it aside. They were not to substitute the animal in front or behind the tenth one. If they did, then they had to give both the tenth one and the one which they had tried to substitute. God took His chances on that tenth animal and expected them to do the same!

The first tenth was to go for the support of the Levites. The tithe from the other tribes was considered the inheritance of the Levites since they did not receive an inheritance of land when Israel settled in Canaan. God's instructions to Moses were: "And unto the children of Levi, behold, I have given all the tithe in Israel for an inheritance, in return for their service of the tent of meeting" (Numbers 18:21).

When the tribe of Levi received the tithe from the other eleven tribes, they in turn were to give a tithe of what they had received to Aaron for the support of his family and the priests. They had not received a land inheritance either. Jehovah spake to Moses saying, "Moreover thou shalt speak unto the Levites, and say unto them, When ye take of the Children

LESSONS IN CHRISTIAN DOCTRINE

of Israel the tithe which I have given you from them for your inheritance, then ye shall offer up a heave-offering of it for Jehovah, a tithe of the tithe . . . and thereof ye shall give Jehovah's heave-offering to Aaron the priest" (Numbers 18: 26 and 28b). Thus we see God's care of His own. Through the division of the land of Canaan, He had provided for the eleven tribes. He provided for the tribe of Levi and the priests as they ministered in the Tabernacle.

2. *The second tithe.* After the first tithe had been taken, Deuteronomy indicates that a second tithe was to be given out of the nine-tenth's remaining. This second tithe was to be used for a sacred meal to be eaten as an act of worship wherever God instructed. Later on the place was Jerusalem because that is where the Tabernacle and later the Temple stood. This tithe apparently was used to finance the various feasts and meals which Jehovah required of His people. The offerer was also supposed to share this meal with the Levites, since he had no inheritance. (Read Deut. 14:22-27; 12:17-19.) If an Israelite lived too far out to carry this tithe with him then he could convert it into money and then purchase the necessary food in Jerusalem (Deut. 14:24-25).

3. The third year tithe. Deuteronomy 14:28-29 says, "At the end of every three years thou shalt bring forth all the tithe of thine increase in the same year, and shalt lay it up within thy gates: and the Levite, because he hath no portion nor inheritance with thee, and the sojourner, and the fatherless, and the widow, that are within thy gates, shall come, and shall eat and be satisfied; that Jehovah thy God may bless thee in all the work of thy hand which thou doest." The Old Testament does not make clear whether this refers to a third tithe every three years or whether the second tithe was used completely for the poor each third year. According to some ancient scholars each third year the second tithe was to be given entirely to the Levites and the poor. But according to Josephus (Antiquities, IV, VIII, 22), the Poor Tithe was actually a third one.

In summary, the Mosaic Law required the Jew to give one-tenth of all his increase each year to support the Levites as they ministered to God in the Tabernacle. The Levites in turn tithed to the priests so that they might have a living. In addition to this, the eleven tribes were to give a second tithe each year for the purpose of religious feasts in Jerusalem in connection with the worship in the Tabernacle or the Temple. Each third year they gave a Poor Tithe. This went to the Levites, widows, orphans, and the poor (Deut. 26:12-13).

V. DIVINE BLESSINGS ON THE TITHE

God's blessings are always commensurate with man's responsibilities. At first glance, it appears that God had required much of the Children of Israel in the amount of giving, but God has never required man to give to Him other than what He has first blessed him with. God told them if they would obey His commandments that He would bless them abundantly. He said, "Blessed shalt thou be in the city, and blessed shalt thou be in the field. Blessed shall be the fruit of thy ground, and the fruit of thy beasts, the increase of thy cattle, and the young of thy flock. Blessed shall be thy basket and thy kneading-trough. Blessed shalt thou be when thou comest in, and blessed shalt thou be when thou goest out" (Deut. 28:3-6). Solomon exhorted the people of his day to "Honor Jehovah with thy substance, and with the first-fruits of all thine increase: So shall thy barns be filled with plenty, And thy vats shall overflow with new wine" (Proverbs 3:9-10).

Perhaps the most familiar of God's promises to Israel is found in Malachi 3:10-12, where God challenged Israel to:

Bring ye the whole tithe into the store-house, that there may be food in my house, and prove me how herewith, saith Jehovah of hosts, if I will not open you the windows of heaven, and pour you out a blessing, that there shall not be room enough to receive it. And I will rebuke the devourer for your sakes, and he shall not destroy the fruits of your ground; neither shall your vine cast its fruit before the time in the field, saith Jehovah of hosts, And all nations shall call you happy; for ye shall be a delightsome land, saith Jehovah of hosts.

God is a loving and a generous God. He is the same today as he was in Israel's day.

QUESTIONS — GIVING

DISCUSSION:

1. What is the first basic principle of Christian giving? _____
_____

2. Write the second principle of Christian giving? _____
_____

3. Summarize the giving required under the Mosaic law.

_____

_____

_____

COMPLETE:

1. For an offering Cain brought _____ and Abel brought _____.

2. List four things the Bible says God owns.

   a. _____ c. _____

   b. _____ d. _____

3. Melchizedek was the king of _____ and _____ of God Mist High.

4. What do these scriptures say God gives us?

   a. James 1:5 _____

   b. Romans 6:23 _____

   c. I Timothy 6:17 _____

5. Israel gave the first tithe to the _____ because they had no _____.

6. List three blessings God promised to Israel in Malachi 3: 10-12.

   a. _____.

   b. _____.

   c. _____.

Lesson Eleven

GIVING IN THE NEW TESTAMENT

I. **The True Nature of Giving.**
   A. It is a grace.
   B. Act of Worship.
      1. Definite Responsibility.
      2. Worship is directed toward God.
   C. It is an act of love.

II. **Reasons for Giving.**
   A. Advance the work of the kingdom.
   B. To develop spirituality in the Christian.
      1. A right attitude toward money.
      2. Develop the Godlike quality of unselfishness.
   C. Future Accountability.

III. **What is the Standard of Christian Liberality?**
   A. God is the only one who can set the standard of liberality.
   B. More is required of the Christian than the Jew.

In the New Testament the subject of giving is very prominent. The sacred writers have far more to say about the correct and incorrect usage of money than they do about baptism and the Lord's Supper combined. One third of our Lord's parables dealt with money. One verse in every six of the Synoptic Gospels deals with money.

I. THE TRUE NATURE OF GIVING

Many people fail to give as they should largely because they do not understand the true nature of giving. Once a sincere Christian sees the full meaning of this part of his Christian life, it then becomes a joy and a blessing to give.

93

LESSONS IN CHRISTIAN DOCTRINE

A. *It is a grace.* In II Corinthians 8:7 Paul speaks of giving as a grace. "But as ye abound in everything, in faith, and utterance, and knowledge, and in all earnestness, and in your love to us, see that ye abound in this grace also." Webster defines grace as "any spiritual gift or attainment." We speak of love, joy, peace as Christian graces. Paul calls them "fruit of the Spirit" (Galatians 5:22). These graces are characteristics or attributes which the Spirit produces in the Christian's life.

A grace is a definite spiritual quality of life which is not inherent in the natural man, but which grows within his heart through the power of the Holy Spirit. Man by nature is selfish. The first law of life is "self-preservation." Man thinks of himself, his family, his needs and desires first. Only as he becomes like God does he begin to put God and others before himself.

This being the case then, man learns to be unselfish and learns to give just like he learns to do other things in the Christian life. When an individual finds himself unable to give freely to God, he should pray that God will enable him to have the right attitude toward his money and to handle it in a Christ-like manner. The ability to give freely, liberally, and with the proper attitude and motives is a spiritual attainment toward which every Christian should strive.

B. *Act of Worship.* Many Christians look upon the offering as sort of a "necessary evil" to keep the bills paid. A preacher said one time, "If I had my way, I would never take an offering." This preacher obviously did not understand the true nature of giving. Instead of being a nuisance the offering is a sublime act of worship to God.

God required all male Jews to attend the three major feasts held each year: passover, pentecost, and the feast of tabernacles. When they came, God said, "and they shall not appear before the Lord empty: every man shall give as he is able, according to the blessing of Jehovah thy God which he hath given thee" (Deut. 16:16-17). These feasts were a part of their worship of Jehovah. He expected them to bring an offering in proportion to their blessings. This was an act of worship.

The same concept is taught in the New Testament. In Acts 2:42, Luke lists the worship of the early church. Along with teaching, the Lord's Supper, and prayer, he adds "fellowship." This same word is translated in Romans 15:26 as "contribution." The word "fellowship" basically means "sharing." This sharing or giving by the New Testament Church was considered by the Holy Spirit to be worship of God.

This is further confirmed in I Cor. 16:2 where Paul instructs the church "Upon the first day of the week let every

94

one of you lay by him in store, as God hath prospered him, that there be no gatherings when I come." On the same day that they worshipped God in prayer, in Bible study, and the Lord's Supper, they were also to worship with their offerings.

To consider Christian giving as a dedicated act of worship is to lift it out of the realm of the unimportant to that of a:

① Definite Responsibility. Too many people view Christian giving as being a minor part of their Christian responsibility. One gives as he feels like it and when convenient. (Many people seldom "feel" like giving.) God told Israel not to appear before Him empty handed. The Christian today should certainly feel the same responsibility. The poet has caught the idea in this verse.

> "What giving again?" I asked in dismay.
> "And must I keep giving and giving away?" ·
> "Oh no," said the angel, looking me through
> "Just give till the Lord stops giving to you."[1]

② Worship is directed toward God. Giving, as an act of worship, should be to God. Many give to support the preacher, to build a building, or to meet some other expense. This, however, is a false concept. One's giving should always be to God. It may be used for some of these purposes but in the heart of the worshipper should be the thought that this is a gift to God.

In the loaf of the Lord's Supper one should see the body of Christ. In the cup the blood of Christ is seen. Perhaps in the bottom of the offering plate should be painted the hand of Christ so that the Christian will be reminded that his offering is given to Christ. The poet said:

> "Give as you would to the Master.
> If you met His loving look;
> Give as you would of your substance
> As if His hand the offering took."[2]

C. *It is an Act of Love.* Love is the greatest motivating power in the world. All Christian service should be primarily motivated by love. Christian giving should also be done because of love. Paul wrote to the church at Corinth and urged them to "show ye therefore unto them in the face of the churches the *proof of your love,* and of our glorying on your behalf" (II Cor. 8:24). God, the same as man, likes some tangible proof of love. This is one way we show it. John says, "My little children, let us not love in word, neither in tongue; but in deed and in truth" (I John 3:18). God can often tell more about our

---

1. Author Unknown
2. Author Unknown

love for Him through the offering plate than by our claims of love for Him.

It seems fitting that the offering plates should be placed on the same table as the Lord's Supper. In the Lord's Supper one sees the greatest picture or evidence of God's love that is known to man. In the offering should be seen at least one evidence of man's love for God. Truly it should be to the Christian a table of love.

In summary, Christian giving is a grace or Christian attainment that God develops in our lives through His Holy Spirit. It is an act of worship of God. It is not an incidental part of our Christian experience, but is a definite act of obedience and worship unto God. It is an act of love motivated by the love of God towards us and springing from the love of God in our hearts. John states it clearly when he says "we love Him, because He first loved us" (I John 4:19).

II. REASONS FOR GIVING

A. *Advance the work of the kingdom.* Man lives in a material world. It takes money or material wealth to carry on God's work in this world. It takes money to support the preaching of the Gospel. Paul commends the Philippian church for their generous support in the preaching of the Gospel. They had sent offerings to him during his work in Thessalonica (Phil. 4:15-16). They had supported him in his preaching in Corinth (II Cor. 11:9). They later sent a gift to him while he was a prisoner in Rome. It takes money to care for the widow and the orphan, to build church buildings, send missionaries, and print Bibles. This reason for giving is apparent to everyone.

B. *To develop spirituality in the Christian.* This purpose for Christian giving is the primary one. The question is asked, Why does God require us to give? The obvious answer is that we might become like Him. It is true that God owns everything. If He chose, He could provide miraculously all the needs that the Church has. This, however, would not develop Christian character and God-likeness in His children. All of God's laws and requirements are for our good. Paul in urging the Corinthians to give, reminded them that God would increase the fruits of their righteousness. "You will be enriched in every way for great generosity" (II Cor. 9:11). Paul indicates in this scripture that God would bless them and enrich them spiritually because they gave.

Jesus says "for where your treasure is there will your heart be also" (Matt. 6:21). Anytime that an individual gives to something he will have more interest in it. This is because his money represents a part of his life. When he has invested his life in something, then he is concerned about it. Jesus understood this principle, that if a man will put his money in the kingdom of God that this will be one means of reaching his heart for the kingdom also. God wants the man not the money. But he uses money to reach the man. In Luke 16:10-12, Jesus teaches that money is a testing ground or a method by which God determines whether man is worthy of spiritual blessings. He states that:

> He that is faithful in very little is faithful also in much: and he that is unrighteous in a very little is unrighteous also in much. If therefore ye have not been faithful in the unrighteous mammon, who will commit to your trust the true riches? And if ye have not been faithful in that which is another's, who will give you that which is your own?

In this scripture money or material wealth is represented by the words "little," "unrighteous mammon," "that which is another's" Spiritual riches are represented by the words "much," "true riches," "that which is your own." Jesus says that if we have not been faithful in our material wealth, if we have not handled them right, then we will not receive the true riches which are spiritual. In other words, when we learn to handle our money right, then God will grant to us the greater spiritual riches which He has in store for us. By the same token, if a Christian fails to pass the test in handling his money, then Jesus indicates that he will not receive great spiritual blessings. It is a true statement that you never see a truly spiritual man who is stingy. The reason being that his stinginess is the block which prevents God from filling his life with true righteousness.

God requires us to give in an effort to instill within us:

1. A right attitude toward money. The Lord wants us to develop the concept that money is our servant, not our master. The poet has said:

> Dug from the mountain side,
> Washed from the glen,
> Servant am I
> Or the master of men.[1]

When a Christian understands that God gives him material blessings to be used for God and good, then his money becomes his servant. Money can be used as a blessing in a thousand ways when it is the servant of a Christian, but when money becomes the master, a tragedy can result. A prime example is the rich young ruler in Mark 10.

---

1. Author Unkownn

97

2. Develop the Godlike quality of unselfishness. There's perhaps no characteristic more foreign to the nature of God than that of selfishness and covetousness. God loved us so much that He gave His Son. God, who gives us richly all things to enjoy, has no trace of selfishness in Him. He asks us to give that we may develop this same spirit within us.

A preacher was asked by the elders to issue a letter from the church office stating that the church was not meeting its budget and urging the members to give more generously. One of the members of the church, highly incensed at receiving the letter, wrote the preacher a sharp reply. He concluded his letter with these words: "It seems to me that all there is to Christianity is give, give, give!"

Wisely the preacher did not answer the letter immediately. Some time later after much thought he wrote the member this note: "Dear Sir: Thank you for writing and giving me the best definition of Christianity that I have ever heard—'give, give, give!' "

The more one studies Christianity the more he realizes that the words "love" and "give" are inseparable and form the basis of true Christian living.

C. *Future Accountability*. Jesus said, "For the Son of man shall come in the glory of his Father with his angels; and then he shall reward every man according to his works" (Matt. 16:27). Paul echoed the words of the Master when he wrote: "For we must all appear before the judgment seat of Christ; that every one may receive the things done in his body, according to that he hath done, whether it be good or bad" (II Cor. 5:10). The Hebrew writer reminds us that "it is appointed unto men once to die but after this the judgment" (Hebrews 9:27). The song writer has expressed the idea of the future judgment and its purpose in this verse: "There is coming a day when to judgment we go, there to reap as in life we have sown, so be careful each day what you do, what you say, for you meet it again by and by."

When the scriptures tell us that we shall give an account of the deeds done here on earth, it is evident that God will examine our giving along with other acts of Christian service. God rebuked the Jews for their greed and accused them of robbing Him. When they asked wherein they had robbed Him, He said "in tithes and offering. Ye are cursed with a curse: for ye have robbed Me, even this whole nation" (Malachi 3:8-9). I am sure that God will be less pleased with the Christian if he robs Him. Paul in Colossians 3:5 speaks of covetousness as being idolatry. This is a serious sin. It was so serious that it cost the rich young ruler his eternal salvation. It is unthinkable that a Christian who has received every blessing imaginable, from God, would in turn rob Him by keeping back material blessings which belong to God. This is both ingratitude and stealing. We must learn to give in the right proportion as well as with the right attitude and motive lest we be condemned at the judgment of God.

On the other hand, when we die, God will entrust to us the true riches of eternity if we have been faithful in the use of our money on earth. We will then hear Him say, "Well done, good and faithful servant; thou hast been faithful over a few things, I will make thee ruler over many things: enter thou into the joy of thy Lord" Matt. 25:23).

John Rutledge was right when he said, "By doing good with his money a man, as it were, stamps the image of God upon it, and makes it pass current for the merchandise of heaven."

III. WHAT IS THE STANDARD OF CHRISTIAN LIBERALITY?

Having seen that giving is a Christian grace, and also a part of our worship of God, the logical question arises, How much should I give? What is liberal giving?

It is evident that man is not qualified to set the standard of liberality. Because some who give 1% of their income believe that they are generous. Others who give 20% feel that they are rendering only a reasonable service to God. Evidently both groups are not right. That would create in the church a situation similar to ancient Israel when "every man did that which was right in his own eyes" (Judges 17:6).

A. *God is the only one who can set the standard of liberality.* In the scriptures there is no maximum amount that a Christian can give. When it comes to how much he can give, the sky is the limit. However, the Bible does indicate a minimum or starting place for Christian giving. In Lesson 10 we see that the Jew in the Old Testament gave a first tithe to support the Lord's work (Lev. 27:30-32; Num. 18:21-28). In addition he gave a second tenth in worship of God (Deut. 12:17-19). The righteous Jew also gave offerings in addition to the tithe (Malachi 3:8).

B. *More is required of the Christian than the Jew.* The New Testament urges the Christian to give liberally (Acts 12:8); to give "bountifully" and cheerfully (II Cor. 9:6, 7). Jesus told his disciples that "Except your righteousness shall exceed the righteousness of the scribes and Pharisees, ye shall in no case enter the kingdom of heaven" (Matt. 5:20).

LESSONS IN CHRISTIAN DOCTRINE

Certainly God does not require less of the Christian than He did of the Jew. Surely the Christian should begin with the tithe and exceed that just as much as His love for God dictates, and the necessities of life permit.

John G. Alber wrote:

> To say that the principle of the tithe has been abolished in Christ is to say that while in everything else Christ has enlarged upon Moses, in this respect the Gospel sounds a retreat; that Christianity has lowered the standard of the virtue of liberality; that with greater blessings than the Jew, the Christian may, if he feels like it, give less for the sake of the world than the Jew gave for the sake of Palestine; that the Jew did more under a loveless law than the Christian under the law of love.
>
> That cold duty calls forth greater sacrifice under the law than gratitude under the gospel; that Sinai is stronger than Calvary; that the outcome is better when Moses sternly drives than when Christ lovingly draws; and that for the sake of the world with all its heathenism and sin we had better return to the "yoke of bondage" of the Old Testament. Such conjecture could not stand the light of reason if there were no revelation.[1]

The Christian has a greater covenant with God (Hebrews 8:6). He has better promises under that covenant (Heb. 8:6; II Peter 1:4). He has a greater commission to carry the Gospel to the whole world (Matt. 16:15-16). The needs are greater. To meet these needs the Christian must give more than the Jew to be pleasing to Christ and to reach the world with the Gospel.

QUESTIONS — GIVING IN THE NEW TESTAMENT

FILL IN THE BLANKS

1. II Cor. 9:6, 7—"But this I say, He which soweth _____

_____ shall reap also sparingly; and he which soweth

_____ shall reap also bountifully. Every man

according as he purposeth in his _____, so let

---

1. Alber, John G., *The Principle of the Tithe*, Lincoln, Nebraska: *Reporter Pub. Co.*, p. 23.

100

GIVING IN THE NEW TESTAMENT

him give; not _____ or of _____

for God loveth a _____ giver."

2. I Cor. 16:2—"Upon the _____ day of the week let everyone of you lay by him in store, as God hath _____ _____ him, that there be no _____ _____ when I come."

3. Matthew 5:20—"For I say unto you, That except your _____ shall _____ the _____ of the scribes and Pharisees, ye shall in no case _____ _____ into the kingdom of heaven."

COMPLETE:

1. Giving is a grace. A grace is _____.

2. List three (3) reasons why the Christian should give.

   a. _____.

   b. _____.

   c. _____.

3. What two (2) ideas are expressed in the statement that giving is an act of worship? _____

_____

_____

4. List all the reasons you can why a Christian should give more under grace than the Jew did under Law.

_____

_____

_____

Lesson Twelve

THE MISSION OF THE CHURCH

I. What is the mission of the church?

II. What does missions mean?

III. Christianity is missionary by nature.
   A. Christianity claims to be the only true religion.
   B. Christianity's view of mankind is that all have sinned and need the salvation which is in Christ.
   C. Christ, the head of the church, was the world's greatest missionary.

IV. Motives for missions.
   A. A keen realization of what we have in Christ and the consciousness of the world's desperate need for it.
   B. The command of Christ.
   C. Gratitude for salvation.

V. Who is responsible for missions?

VI. Methods for missions.
   A. Selection of preaching points.
   B. Preaching and Prayer.
   C. Paul established indigenous churches.

I.   WHAT IS THE MISSION OF THE CHURCH?

The purpose of the church is expressed clearly and briefly in Matthew 28:19-20. It is two-fold. First, the church is to teach all men concerning Christ, and bring them to saving faith in Him. Then they are to baptize them into Christ (Matt.

THE MISSION OF THE CHURCH

28:19). Secondly, the church is to continue to teach these obedient believers until they are built up and established in Him (Matt. 28:20). This is the only task the church has; the only reason for its existence. Its mission is to bring men to Christ and to build them into the image of Christ. This program is world wide. It continues as long as one soul is lost. We can say then that the evangelization of the world is the mission of the church.

II. WHAT DOES MISSIONS MEAN?

The most frequently used term for this world evangelism is the term missions. What do we mean by missions? The dictionary defines the noun "mission" as "the act of sending, or state of being sent, with certain powers, to do some special service;—a calling, especially to preach and spread a religion." The term "missions" is not in the New Testament. It came from the Latin word, "*Mitto*," "I send." A missionary is a "sent-one" or "one sent on a mission." It is synonymous with "apostle" (from the Greek, *Apostello*, "I send"). The word "missions" is a modern term for the great purpose of the church—world wide evangelism.

III. CHRISTIANITY IS MISSIONARY BY NATURE

The question is often asked, Why send missionaries to other lands when they already have a religion? What is the justification for sending millions of dollars and thousands of missionaries, to convert other nations to Christianity? Would it not be better to leave them alone where they are and not disturb them with this new teaching? If Christianity is just *a* religion among many religions and if Christ is *a* Saviour among many Saviours then there would be little point in going. If this is true, then there would be other ways of salvation open to them.

The justification for world missions is in the very nature of Christianity itself. There are at least two major things that make Christianity missionary. These are its exclusive claims and its view of mankind.

A. *Christianity claims to be the only true religion.* This claim brought it into conflict with the Romans of the first century and continues to create resentment among unbelievers today. The Romans would gladly have given it a place among the many religions of the empire but they objected to the exclusiveness of the Christian faith. They resented its saying that all other religions were false.

There is no doubt that the New Testament claims exclusiveness for its message. Jehovah is not *a* God; He is *the* only

103

God. Paul says, "we know that an idol is nothing in the world, and that there is none other God but one" (I Cor. 8:4). Jesus Christ is not *a* Saviour; He is *the only* Saviour of men. Speaking of Jesus, Peter said, "there is no other name under heaven given among men, whereby we must be saved" (Acts 4:12). This is why Christianity is missionary. "If the gospel is *the only* message that can offer men eternal life—then how can I keep quiet? Can I rejoice in my salvation, knowing that others are dying without that salvation? Must I not feel as Paul did when he wrote to the Romans, 'I am a debtor . . . to preach the gospel to you' (Romans 1:14-15)?"[1]

B. *Christianity's view of mankind is that all have sinned and need the salvation which is in Christ.* Salvation means to be saved from sin and from the results of sin. There was a firm belief that sin had alienated the whole world from God by corrupting the nature of man and had brought condemnation and death. "All have sinned" (Romans 3:23) and no one can save himself from it. Only in Christ can salvation from sin be found. This belief was the compelling force that sent the early Christians away from home and family to face hardship, persecution, and death to carry this saving message to those dying in sin. These two beliefs of the church make Christianity missionary by its very nature.

C. *Christ, the head of the church, was the world's greatest missionary.* A third reason for missions is the example of Christ. Jesus not only taught missions, and commanded missions, but He Himself was the greatest missionary in history. John wrote, "God sent His only begotten Son into the world, that we might believe through Him" (I John 4:9). Jesus Christ then was a missionary, a "sent one." He was sent from heaven to earth with a definite purpose. The Lord told what that purpose was when He said, "the Son of man is come to seek and to save that which was lost" (Luke 19:10). Again He said, "I came down from heaven not to do my own will but the will of him that sent me" (John 6:38). His purpose was the same as any missionary today. He was sent to save those who were lost—"dead in trespasses and sins" (Eph. 2:1). When we do missionary work today, we are continuing the great program begun by our Lord when He left heaven and came to earth to make salvation possible for all men.

IV. MOTIVES FOR MISSIONS

A motive is something that prompts one to act. It is a force that moves or impells one to do something. What are the proper motives for going as a missionary or in sending others?

1. Cook, Harold, R., *An Introduction to the Study of Christian Missions*, page 23.

THE MISSION OF THE CHURCH

There are many motives which tug at the heart of the true believer but we will mention only a few.

A. *A keen realization of what we have in Christ and the consciousness of the world's desperate need for it.* When a man truly sees Christ and understands what He has done for him, he can never be happy until he shares Him with another. When one realizes that he cannot live without Christ, then he can not bear to think of other men living without Him. After having tasted of the water of life, he can not stand idly by and see another die for lack of this same water. Herein lies one of the greatest motives for world evangelism.

If a Christian will look at the cross of Calvary until the true meaning of what Christ did there is clear, then he can never be selfish with the message of love expressed in Christ.

This is the meaning of John 3:16. God so loved that He gave His Son to save lost men. Jesus loved and gave His life as a ransom for them. (Rom. 5:6-8.) We today as God's children must continue this search until every lost brother of ours and child of God is found and brought safely back to his heavenly Father.

B. *The command of Christ.* Jesus not only taught and practiced missions, He also commanded it. All four Gospels and the Acts give the great commission in one form or another. Matthew 28:18-20 says, "And Jesus came to them and spake unto them, saying, All authority hath been given unto me in heaven and on earth. Go ye therefore, and make disciples of all nations, baptizing them unto the name of the Father and of the Son and of the Holy Spirit: teaching them to observe all things whatsoever I commanded you: and lo, I am with you always, even unto the end of the world." Mark recorded it in a somewhat shorter form. "And he said unto them, Go ye into all the world, and preach the gospel to the whole creation. He that believeth and is baptized shall be saved; but he that disbelieveth shall be condemned" (Mark 16:15-16). Luke gives the commission in these words, "And he said unto them, Thus it is written, that the Christ should suffer, and rise again from the dead the third day; and that repentance and remission of sins should be preached in his name unto all the nations, beginning from Jerusalem" (Luke 24:46-49). John tells us that when Christ first appeared to His disciples after His resurrection he said, "as my Father hath sent me, even so send I you" (John 20:21). Again in Acts 1:8 we have another expression of the same command. "But ye shall receive power, when the Holy Spirit is come upon you: and ye shall be my witnesses both in Jerusalem, and in all Judea and Samaria, and unto the uttermost part of the earth."

LESSONS IN CHRISTIAN DOCTRINE

For one who has never acknowledged the Lordship of Christ, His commandment has no force. But if one has wholeheartedly submitted to the authority of Christ, he will find his greatest pleasure in earnestly carrying out His will. He will rejoice in the honor of being an ambassador for Christ, seeking to reconcile man to God (II Cor. 5:18-20).

The believer should obey the Lord's command simply because of who He is: the head of the church, the Lord of Lords and the King of Kings. It should be a joyous privilege to do so. However, there is the added motive of judgment, if one does not obey. Many people think they can have their Christianity "with or without missions." Many church leaders will simply dismiss the subject with the statement, "I do not believe in missions." Others will neglect to do a thing about it just as though Christ had never spoken or given a command.

Many Christians would shrink from the thought of leaving out the command of baptism in the great commission, yet will freely ignore the part where Jesus says "go ye into all the world" (Mark 16:15). The same Lord that commanded baptism, also commanded that the Gospel be carried to the entire world. Man has not been given the privilege of obeying part of the Lord's command and ignoring the rest. He does this at his own peril.

In II Cor. 5:10, Paul speaks of his appearance before the judgment seat of Christ to give an account of his life. He then says, "knowing therefore the terror of the Lord, we persuade men" (II Cor. 5:11). With Paul, his preaching the gospel was not simply a matter of choice. The Lord had spoken. Knowing the terror of the Lord upon the disobedient, he feared not to obey. He further clarifies his feelings when he says, "For if I preach the gospel, I have nothing to glory of; for necessity is laid upon me; for woe is unto me, if I preach not the gospel" (I Cor. 9:16). Christians today *must* regain this holy fear of God, and evangelize the world, or face His wrath at the judgment.

C. *Gratitude for Salvation.* The newspapers reported the story of a man who had been healed of a dread disease by a doctor. In an effort to express his undying love and gratitude to the doctor, he rented a large bill-board on a main highway. On it, in large letters, he placed the doctor's name and told the story of his healing.

The sinner who has been healed of the malady of sin, by God's grace, should never cease to tell the world of the saving grace that is in Christ, our great physician. This should be a compelling motive for missions. We are saved to save others. Paul says, "I am debtor . . . so much as in me is, I am ready to preach the Gospel" (Romans 1:14-15).

106

THE MISSION OF THE CHURCH

V. WHO IS RESPONSIBLE FOR MISSIONS?

Jesus gave the great commission to the Apostles. However, it was not theirs alone to carry out. The early church clearly understood that it was the task of every believer.

Philip was one of the first deacons but he became such an effective preacher that he was later called "Philip the Evangelist" (Acts 21:8). When the church was scattered from Jerusalem following the death of Stephen, it says "therefore they that were scattered abroad went everywhere preaching the word" (Acts 8:4). This was not the Apostles, for they remained in Jerusalem (Acts 8:1). These were the members of the church. Every believer was a preacher in the true sense of the word. In Revelation 22:17 is recorded Christ's last great commission to his disciples. "And the Spirit and the bride say, Come. And he that heareth, let him say, Come. And he that is athirst, let him come: he that will, let him take the water of life freely." Everyone that hears, in the sense of believing and accepting, is to immediately begin calling others to the water of life.

Who is to do missionary work? Every Christian is, individually and corporately as the church. Every Christian should feel a sense of divine mission to both go and send. He should first go to those in his own neighborhood. The Lord may also call him to go to other lands. If he does not go to foreign lands, then he should do his utmost to provide for those who do go. The Lord will not ask at the judgment, "What did your church do for missions?" But will ask, "What did *you* do?" Until *each* believer feels this *personal* responsibility, the world will not be won for Christ.

> "Lord, Thou hast giv'n to me a trust,
> A high and holy dispensation,
> To tell the world, and tell I must,
> The story of Thy great salvation;
> Thou might'st have sent from heav'n above
> Angelic hosts to tell the story,
> But in Thy condescending love,
> On men Thou hast conferred the glory.

> "Let me be faithful to my trust,
> Telling the world the story;
> Press on my heart the woe,
> Put in my feet the go;
> Let me be faithful to my trust,
> And use me for Thy glory."[1]

---

1. Quoted in *The Bible Basis of Missions*, Robert Hall Glover, Bible House of Los Angeles, 1946, page 208.

VI. METHODS FOR MISSIONS.

The mention of missionary methods immediately calls to mind the book of Acts. In this book, God has furnished His church with the finest textbook on missions in existence. One writer speaks of Acts as "the authorized Missionary Manual of the church."[2]

Books have been written on the missionary methods contained in Acts. The mention of a few will suffice for this study.

A. *Selection of preaching points.* Paul did not seemingly lay out his entire itinerary on a tour but rather left room for the Holy Spirit to guide him. However, there is a pattern to Paul's preaching points on his tours.

Wherever possible the Apostle Paul followed Roman roads. The reason being that over these roads flowed the stream of commerce from one important city to another. Paul chose cities because of their strategic importance for trade, politics, or education. Antioch, of Syria, for instance, had a population of about 500,000. It was the third metropolis of the Mediterranean world and was the home of the Imperial legate of Syria. This was an ideal place for Paul to concentrate his efforts because of the great influence this city could have on the world about it.

Cyprus, though a small island, provided an excellent starting point for evangelization because it lay within easy reach of three continents and was a convenient center of trade. Corinth was the commercial and political capital of the province of Asia. Here Paul spent nearly three years. Paul would plant the church in central strategic locations. He then left the local church to evangelize surrounding areas.

B. *Preaching and prayer.* When Paul had chosen a field of labor he then proceeded to establish a church by preaching and teaching (cf. Acts 14:1; 17:1-3, 17; 18:5; 19:8-9). Paul knew of no way for lost men to be saved except through the medium of preaching. He told the Corinthians, "It was God's good pleasure through the foolishness of the preaching to save them that believe" (I Cor. 1:21). This preaching was essential to produce faith. "So belief cometh of hearing, and hearing by the word of Christ" (Rom. 10:17). In Romans 10:14 he expresses the vital need for preaching as he wrote, "But how are men to call upon him in whom they have not believed? And how are they to believe in him of whom they have never heard? And how are they to hear without a preacher?" To Paul, preaching was the means chosen of God to bring men to Christ and establish churches.

---

2. Glover, *The Bible Basis of Missions*, page 26

THE MISSION OF THE CHURCH

Prayer was another chief method used by Paul. Throughout his letters, he asked for the prayers of his fellow Christians and assured them of his prayers for them. He asked for prayers for the spread of the gospel (II Thes. 3:1); for his deliverance from great perils (II Cor. 1:10-11); that the Jewish Christians in Jerusalem might accept the offerings of the Gentiles (Rom. 15:30-31); and that he might be given the opportunity to preach the gospel message (Col. 4:3). He also assured his converts that he was in continual prayer for them (Phil. 1:3-5).

Paul depended on his personal prayer life as the driving force of his life. He used prayer as a method because it unfailingly brought results for the advancement of the kingdom.

C. *Paul established indigenous churches.* By indigenous is meant that the church was self-governing, self-supporting, and self-propagating.

1. Self-governing. From the study of Acts we learn that Paul did not oversee the church any longer than was necessary to develop leadership. This is evident on his first missionary tour. Paul and Barnabas established churches in Antioch of Pisidia, Iconium, Lystra, and Derbe. As they returned confirming and exhorting the churches, Luke records, "and when they had appointed elders for them in every church, with prayer and fasting, they committed them to the Lord in whom they believed" (Acts 14:23). In Acts 20 we note there were elders in the church at Ephesus (cf. Phil. 1:1). Titus is instructed to appoint elders in every city on the island of Crete (Titus 1:5). These local leaders continued the teaching and overseeing of the church while Paul moved to another field.

2. Self-supporting. Self-support was the second principle followed by Paul. By self-support is meant that the individual church took care of its own financial needs. There are instances of one church lending assistance to a sister congregation when they were in need. For example, Antioch sent relief to Jerusalem (Acts 11:27-30). Paul collected benevolent gifts throughout Asia and Greece for the poor saints in Judea (I Cor. 16:1, 2; Romans 15:31). However, there is no evidence that a church received money for their regular expenses.

Paul instructed the churches in Galatia to support those who taught them the word. "Let him who received instruction in the Word (of God) share all good things with his teacher—contributing to his support" (Galatians 6:6, Amplified). Paul writes to Timothy, "Let the elders who rule well be considered worthy of double honor, especially those who labor in preaching and teaching" (I Tim. 5:17, RSV). This principle of self-support should receive careful attention today. Considerable

LESSONS IN CHRISTIAN DOCTRINE

harm can be done by making the native church dependent for its existence on the money supplied by the missionaries. It can rob the native Christians of spiritual growth and blessings derived from a life of faith. It can cause the church to shirk its responsibility for the local work. If, however, they are properly taught and given the responsibility for their own affairs, they will usually respond in a commendable way. It certainly worked in the first century. It should work in the twentieth.

3. Self-propagation. This principle is dependent to a great extent upon the enactment of the previous two. For when a church is not self-governing and self-supporting, it rarely is self-reproducing. This principle is very evident in the New Testament is as seen, for example, in the Tesssalonian brethren. Paul says, "For not only has the word of the Lord sounded forth from you in Macedonia and Achaia, but your faith in God has gone forth everywhere, so that we need not say anything" (I Thess. 1:8). In the majority of cases the native workers can win their own people much faster than a foreigner can. The other vital fact is that when Paul taught these churches to evangelize those around them, he was enlisting every Christian in the work of the ministry and not just a few paid workers. This is teaching the whole church to minister (Ephesians 4:11-12). This principle is also valid and necessary today.

QUESTIONS — THE MISSION OF THE CHURCH

COMPLETE:

1. Why is Christianity missionary by its very nature?

_____

_____

_____

2. What type of cities did Paul choose to plant new churches?

_____

_____

3. What, to you, is the greatest motive for doing missionary work?

_____

_____

4. List the three (3) characteristics of an indigenous church.

a. _____

b. _____

c. _____

5. How would you answer this objection: "The great commission was given only to the Apostles. I am not responsible

for it." _____

_____

_____

_____

DEFINE THESE WORDS:

1. Missionary—

2. Indigenous—

3. Mission—

4. Motive—

5. Commission—

Lesson Thirteen

THE COMING OF THE LORD

I. The Certainity of His Coming.
   A. Some doubt His return.
   B. The evidence for His coming.
      1. By Jesus Himself.
      2. The testimony of angels.
      3. The testimony of the Apostles.
      4. Proof from type.
      5. The witness of the Lord's Supper.

II. The Manner of His Coming.
   A. Visibly.
   B. With the clouds.
   C. In Glory with the angels.
   D. In convulsions of physical nature.

III. The Time of His Coming.

IV. The Christian's Response to His Coming.
   A. Separation from the world.
   B. A personal holiness.
      1. Sincerity.
      2. Sobriety.
      3. Unselfishness.
      4. Patience.
      5. Faithfulness.
   C. Watchfulness.
   D. Working.

THE COMING OF THE LORD

There is no truth in the Bible more important than that of our Lord's return to earth. His first coming was to obtain salvation for man. The second coming will be to receive those who through faith and obedience have obtained that salvation (Hebrews 7:28).

The importance of this doctrine is seen in the attention and emphasis given to the second coming in the Word of God. One man has estimated that one-fifth of the entire New Testament is directly concerned with the Lord's return. Four of Jesus' parables teach concerning it. One illustration of this emphasis is in the First Thessalonian letter. Paul concludes each chapter with a reference to the Lord's return (I Thess. 1:10; 2:19; 3:13; 4:15-18; 5:23). Paul referred to it so often that they concluded that the second coming was immediate. He wrote II Thessalonians to correct this view.

One cannot read the New Testament without sensing the vital spot this doctrine occupied in the thinking of the early church.

I. THE CERTAINTY OF HIS COMING

A. *Some doubt His return.* Nothing is more clearly taught in the New Testament than that Christ will come again. This is the great expectation of all true Christians. Yet there are some who do not believe that He is coming again in person to the earth. Peter foretold that there would be such men on the earth. The Apostle said, "in the last days mockers shall come with mockery, walking after their own lusts, and saying, Where is the promise of his coming? for, from the day that the fathers fell asleep, all things continue as they were from the beginning of the creation" (II Peter 3b, 4).

Because the Lord delays His coming, many have concluded that He will not come. The evil servant made the same erroneous conclusion to his everlasting sorrow in the parable which Jesus gave in Matthew 24:45-51.

In addition to those who reject Christ's personal return there are others who try to explain it away. One group of religious leaders believe that as Christ's gospel reaches more people that in some sense this is the fulfillment of His promised return. The only coming of Christ as they see it, is when He comes into the hearts of each individual. This is not the teaching of the New Testament.

Another group insists that Jesus came in a spiritual sense in 1914. The Bible teaches that Christ returned in the Spirit on the day of Pentecost (Acts 2). Jesus told His Apostles, "Lo, I am with you always, even unto the end of the world" (Matt. 28:20). Jesus had also said, "If any man love me, he will keep

113

my word: and my Father will love him, and we will come unto him, and make our abode with him" (John 14:23). Christ has been with His church spiritually speaking all the time. The second coming as taught in the Bible is a personal, visible coming.

B. *The evidence for His coming.* There is no lack of evidence that Jesus will come to earth again. Hebrews 10:37 states, "He that shall come *will come*, and will not tarry." The prophecy of His second coming antedates even His first advent, being prophesied by Daniel in the Old Testament. "I saw in the night visions, and there came with the clouds of heaven one like unto a son of man, and he came even to the ancient of days, and they brought him near before him" (Daniel 7:13). The references to it in the Old Testament are few and somewhat obscure. It remained for the New Testament to clarify this great event. The first proof of His coming is given:

1. By Jesus Himself. He told the Sanhedrin, "Henceforth ye shall see the Son of man sitting at the right hand of Power, and coming on the clouds of heaven" (Matt. 26:64). Earlier, He had expressed the same promise to the disciples saying, "Then shall appear the sign of the Son of man in heaven: and then shall all the tribes of the earth mourn, and they shall see the Son of man coming on the clouds of heaven with power and great glory" (Matt. 24:30). His best loved promise is found in John 14:3, "And if I go and prepare a place for you, I come again, and will receive you unto myself; that where I am, there ye may be also." Many years after Jesus had returned to heaven, He flashed this reassuring news to earth through the pen of the Apostle John, "Behold, I come quickly; and my reward is with me, to render to each man according as his work is" (Rev. 22:12). The very last message in the Bible is, "He who testifieth these things saith, Yea: I come quickly. Amen: come, Lord Jesus" (Rev. 22:20). Jesus said, "Heaven and earth shall pass away, but my words shall not pass away" (Matt. 24:35). Jesus said He would come again. We can be sure that Christ will keep His word.

2. The testimony of angels. As the Apostles stood on the Mount of Olives watching their beloved Lord ascend into heaven, suddenly their minds were drawn back to earth by the appearance of two men—evidently angels—in white apparel, who said, "Ye men of Galilee, why stand ye looking into heaven? this Jesus, who was received up from you into heaven, shall so come in like manner as ye beheld him going into heaven" (Acts 1:11). The scriptures tell us that the angels will accompany Him on His return. Certainly they should know about it and their testimony is trustworthy.

THE COMING OF THE LORD

3. The testimony of the Apostles. The Apostle Peter is very emphatic as to the Lord's return as he refutes those who deny it (II Peter 3:1-14). Peter tells us that the Lord is not slack concerning His promise to return but is long suffering, not wishing that any should perish but that all should come to repentance. Then he says, "But the day of the Lord will come as a thief; in the which the heavens shall pass away with a great noise, and the elements shall be dissolved with fervent heat, and the earth and the works that are therein shall be burned up" (II Peter 3:10; cf. Acts 3:19-21; I Peter 1:3-13; 4:12, 13; 5:4).

John adds his voice to the many witnesses to Christ's return by saying, "Behold, he cometh with the clouds; and every eye shall see him, and they that pierced him; and all the tribes of the earth shall mourn over him. Even so, Amen" (Revelation 1:7). He further exhorts the Christians to "Abide in Him; that, if he shall be manifested, we may have boldness, and not be ashamed before him at his coming" (I John 2:28). John also reveals this wonderful thought when he says, "Beloved, now are we children of God, and it is not yet made manifest what we shall be. We know that, if he shall be manifested, we shall be like him; for we shall see him even as he is" (I John 3:2).

The Apostle Paul, more than the other Apostles, taught and rejoiced in the fact of the Lord's return. The glorious appearing of the Lord Jesus Christ, was "the blessed hope" toward which Paul ever directed the minds of his readers. "Ye yourselves know perfectly," said Paul, "that the day of the Lord so cometh as a thief in the night" (I Thess. 5:1-11). "The Lord Himself shall descend from heaven with a shout, with the voice of the archangel, and with the trumpet of God" (4:13-17). "As it is appointed unto men once to die, but after this the judgment: so Christ was once offered to bear the sins of many; and unto them that look for Him shall He appear the second time without sin unto salvation" (Heb. 9:27-28; cf. Acts 17:30-31; Rom. 2:16; 8:16-25; 13:11; I Cor. 1:7; 4:5; 11:26; 15:23, 50-52; Phil. 2:16; 3:20; Col. 3:1-4; I Thess. 1:9-10; 2:19; 3:11-13; II Thess. 1:7-12; 2:1-10; II Tim. 4:6-8; Titus 2:13; Rev. 6:12-17; 14:14-15; 16:15-21; 20:7-15).

4. Proof from type. God filled the Old Testament with shadows or dim reflections of events and institutions that would appear in the New Testament. These foreshadowings are called types. Many of these types are to be found in the Tabernacle. Aaron, the first High Priest of the Tabernacle, was a type of Christ, who is our High Priest (Hebrews 4:14). Once a year on the Day of Atonement, Aaron would enter the

Holy of Holies with the blood of animals, to make atonement for the sins of Israel. Following this he would come back to the people and pronounce a blessing upon them with the assurance that their sins had been taken away by the atonement made on the Mercy Seat (cf. Numbers 6:24-26).

Our great High Priest did not make an atonement for us upon a Mercy Seat here on earth but has entered "into heaven itself, now to appear in the presence of God for us" (Heb. 9:24). Christ having offered Himself as a sacrifice to put away sin, now waits for His second return to earth to redeem those who are His. The Hebrew writer states it like this, "So Christ also, having been once offered to bear the sins of many, shall appear a second time, apart from sin, to them that wait for him, unto salvation" (Hebrews 9:28). Since Christ has fulfilled the first part of this type, we are certain He will complete the second part.

5. The witness of the Lord's Supper. We normally think of the Lord's Supper as pointing back to Calvary. Like the cross, the Lord's Supper also points in two directions. It is God's signpost pointing back to Calvary and forward to His return. Paul told the Corinthians, "For as often as ye eat this bread, and drink the cup, ye proclaim the Lord's death till he come" (I Cor. 11:26). Each Lord's day, as the Christian meditates on Calvary and the love of God as seen in the sacrifice of Christ, he should also look forward to his complete redemption when Christ comes again. Each week the saints of God should remind themselves that they are one week nearer the Lord's return. This should be a joy and a strength to keep them faithful to the end. This thought should also awaken one to the brevity of time and the need for earnest effort in saving lost souls.

With all this assurance that Jesus will come again, we can rest our souls with the Apostle Peter who said, "For we did not follow cunningly devised fables, when we made known unto you the power and coming of our Lord Jesus Christ, but we were eyewitnesses of his majesty" (II Peter 1:16). And heed his further advice when he says, "Wherefore girding up the loins of your mind, be sober and set your hope perfectly on the grace that is to be brought unto you at the revelation of Jesus Christ" (I Peter 1:13).

II. THE MANNER OF HIS COMING.

The scripture also gives much detail as to the manner of the Lord's return. Here are a few descriptions of His coming.

A. *Visibly.* The angels told the Apostles "this Jesus, who was received up from you into heaven, shall so come in like manner *as ye beheld him going into heaven*" (Acts 1:11).

116

THE COMING OF THE LORD

They had been standing on the Mount of Olives talking to Him. As He lifted up His hands to bless them, His feet lifted from the ground and He began to ascend toward Heaven. As He moved upward, a bright cloud received Him out of their sight (Luke 24:50, 51; Acts 1:9). The Apostles were talking to Him, and they saw Him depart and go toward Heaven. They continued to look as long as they could catch a glimpse of Him. The scripture says that He will come again in like manner. Revelation 1:7 says, "Behold, he cometh with clouds; and every eye shall see him and they also which pierced Him." One will not need to guess about His coming. Jesus said it would be "as the lightning cometh forth from the east, and is seen even unto the west; so shall be the coming of the Son of man" (Matt. 24:27). Those living on earth will see Him!

B. *With the clouds.* Clouds have always had a special place in God's redemptive work. God came down on Mount Sinai in a cloud (Ex. 24:16). He also came down on the Mount of Transfiguration in a cloud (Matt. 17:5). Israel was led through the wilderness with a cloud by day and a pillar of fire by night (Ex. 13:21). Psalms 104:3 speaks of God "who maketh the clouds his chariot." Jesus left in a cloud. He will return on one. "They shall see the Son of Man coming in the clouds of heaven with power and great glory" (Matt. 24:30). One man said that each time he saw a bright cumulus cloud in the heavens, he found himself subconsciously searching it for the face of His Master. The clouds should be a silent reminder that Jesus is coming again.

C. *In Glory with the angels.* "But when the Son of man shall come in his glory, and all the angels with him, then shall he sit on the throne of his glory" (Matt. 25:31). When Jesus comes again it will be the triumphant march of a conquering king. "For the Lord himself shall descend from heaven, with a shout, with the voice of the archangel, and with the trump of God: and the dead in Christ shall rise first" (I Thess. 4:16). II Thess. 1:7 says, "The Lord Jesus shall be revealed from heaven with His mighty angels." Jesus came the first time as a babe in Bethlehem. He came quietly and unobserved by most of the earth. The second time will be as a king and all the earth will know it. The first time He came in humility, the second time will be glorious. He will be accompanied by the hosts of heaven. His ride into Jerusalem on the donkey is called the "Triumphal Entry." His second coming will truly be the Lord's "Triumphant Re-entry" to this earth.

Paul tells us that Jesus will descend from heaven with a "shout" (I Thess. 4:16). This is translated "a cry of command" (RSV); "a loud cry of summons" (Amplified). Exactly what this cry or shout is, we do not know. Some have thought that it is the shouts of the heavenly host coming with Jesus. This scripture also says there will be the "voice of the archangel" or the "archangel's call." The archangel may be calling the company of the redeemed to join their redeemer (Matt. 24:31). This evidently refers to those who will be alive when Jesus returns.

Paul states that Christ's coming will be heralded by the trumpet of God. Paul calls it "the last trump" and adds, "for the trumpet shall sound, and the dead shall be raised incorruptible, and we shall be changed" (I Cor. 15:52). As the voice of the archangel calls those who are alive, the trumpet may be used to raise the saints from the dead (cf. John 5:28-29). Together they will be caught up together in the clouds "to meet the Lord in the air: and so shall we ever be with the Lord" (I Thess. 4:17).

D. *In Convulsions of physical nature.* The earth itself shall respond to the coming of its creator. Jesus said, "But immediately after the tribulation of those days the sun shall be darkened, and the moon shall not give her light, and the stars shall fall from heaven, and the powers of the heavens shall be shaken: and then shall appear the sign of the Son of man in heaven . . ." (Matt. 24:29). Romans 8:19-22, describes nature as longing for the time when it will be set free from its bondage to decay and enjoy a new freedom. This no doubt is realized in the new earth Peter mentions (II Peter 3:13).

III. THE TIME OF HIS COMING

Since the day that Christ ascended to the Father, men have been speculating as to the time of His return. The Christians in Thessalonica were so sure that He would come in their lifetime, that some seem to have quit work (II Thess. 2-3). William Miller set the date for His coming as 1843. Pastor Charles I. Russell said it would be in 1914. Obviously all these dates were in error. A few years ago a special assistant to the Postmaster General, in Washington, D.C., received a call asking that he issue a commemorative stamp for the second coming of Christ. He was dumbfounded by the unusual request. However, he answered: "If you will tell me the exact time and place, I'll be ready with the issue." The caller hung up.

When the newspapers published this incident, the post office department received a dozen letters from readers saying they knew the time and place. However, the stamp was never issued because the dates ranged from July 1961 to the year 2061!

THE COMING OF THE LORD

The Bible is very clear as to the certainty of His return. The one thing that is not revealed is the *time* of His return. The Lord settled this question of setting dates when He said: "But of that day and that hour knoweth no man, no, not the angels which are in heaven, neither the Son, but the Father" (Mk. 13:32). If the angels in heaven do not know, neither the Son, it is certain that no man knows. Jesus told the Apostles, "It is not for you to know the times or the seasons, which the Father hath put in his own power" (Acts 1:7). All that man needs to know is how to be ready for the Lord's return.

IV. THE CHRISTIAN'S RESPONSE TO HIS COMING

In view of the certainty of Christ's return, the question should be asked: what should be the Christian's response to this? It is obvious that if one honestly believes this doctrine, it will have a powerful effect upon his life and thinking. Undoubtedly the reason why many who profess to believe it and yet are so apathetic, is that in reality they do *not* believe it. The scriptures teach that this doctrine truly believed will produce many blessed changes in the life of the Christian. Here are some of them:

A. *Separation from the world.* Paul exhorts Titus that the Gospel of Christ teaches the "denying ungodliness and worldly lusts, we should live soberly, righteously, and godly, in this present world; looking for that blessed hope, and the glorious appearing of the great God and our Saviour Jesus Christ" (Titus 2:12, 13). Peter makes the same application when he says in II Peter 3:11, "Seeing then that all these things shall be dissolved, what manner of persons ought ye to be in all holy conversation and godliness." John says almost the same thing in I John 2:15-17. As he speaks of the second coming when "the world passeth away and the lust thereof" he calls upon Christians to "love not the world, neither the things that are in the world."

This is a logical response to the second coming doctrine. If "the earth and the works that are therein shall be burned up" it is obvious that man should not cling to that which God has consigned to destruction.

Therefore, we are directed to regard the world as under divine condemnation, and to distinctly separate ourselves from it. The prudent person steers clear of a condemned building, knowing it is dangerous. So ought God's saints to dissociate themselves from the sinful world. They know that the wrath of God is against it, and have been apprised beforehand

119

LESSONS IN CHRISTIAN DOCTRINE

that it is destined for destruction at Christ's return. 'Remember Lot's wife' (Luke 17:20-37).[1]

B. *A Personal Holiness.* Peter says, "Wherefore, beloved, seeing that ye look for such things, be diligent that ye may be found of him in peace, without spot, and blameless" (II Peter 3:14). John reasons along the same principle when he says, "Beloved, now are we the sons of God, and it doth not yet appear what we shall be: but we know that, when he shall appear, we shall be like Him; for we shall see him as he is" (I John 3:2). As the practical application of this hope, he then remarks: "and every man that hath this hope in him purifieth himself, even as he is pure" (I John 3:3).

Negatively, our response to Christ's return should be to repudiate all worldly lust. Positively, we should "live soberly, righteously, and Godly in this present world," as we anticipate "that blessed hope" (Titus 2:12-13).

The expectancy of Christ's return is the motivation for all phases of Christian living. We list a few:

(a) Sincerity. Paul prays that the Philippians "may approve the things that are excellent; that ye may be sincere and void of offence unto the day of Christ; being filled with the fruits of righteousness, which are through Jesus Christ, unto the glory and praise of God" (Philippians 1:10, 11).

(b) Sobriety. Paul reminds the Thessalonians that "the day of the Lord so cometh as a thief in the night . . . therefore let us not sleep, as do others; but let us watch and be sober" (I Thess. 5:2, 6). Evidently the term sober in this connection means sober as opposed to being drunk. It is horrible to contemplate that a person would be drunk on the great occasion of the Lord's coming; yet the Lord also warned against this awful sin as He said, "and take heed to yourselves, lest at any time your hearts be overcharged with surfeiting, and *drunkenness*, and cares of this life, and so that day come upon you unawares" (Luke 21:34). What horror to be found in such a state at His coming! The Christian watching for his Lord will be sober.

(c) Unselfishness (gentleness, forbearance). Paul exhorts the Philippians to "let all men know and perceive and recognize your unselfishness—your considerateness, your forbearing spirit. The Lord is near—He is coming soon" (Philippians 4:5, Amplified).

(d) Patience. The Hebrew writer says, "for ye have need of patience, that, after ye have done the will of God, ye might receive the promise. For yet a little while, and he that shall come will come, and will not tarry" (Heb. 10:36, 37). This

1. Blakely, Fred O., *The Apostls' Doctrine*, Volume I, Page 159.

patience is a stedfastness, an enduring to the end, waiting for His coming. In this same connection, Peter urges the Christians to endure trials and persecution that "the trial of your faith, being much more precious than of gold that perisheth, though it be tried with fire, might be found unto praise and honor and glory at the appearing of Jesus Christ" (I Peter 1:7).

(e) Faithfulness. The coming of the Lord is held as an incentive to faithfulness on the part of Elders in shepherding God's flock, the church. "And when the chief Shepherd shall appear, ye shall receive a crown of glory that fadeth not away" (I Peter 5:4).

C. *Watchfulness.* At least 50 times the New Testament calls upon the church to "watch" for the Lord's return. "Watch therefore: for ye know not on what day your Lord cometh" (Matt. 24:42). "Watch therefore, for ye know not the day nor the hour" (Matt. 25:13). "What I say unto you I say unto all, watch" (Mark 13:37). Peter echoes his Lord's words when he insists that the Christian should always be "looking for and earnestly desiring the coming of the day of God" (II Peter 3:12; cf. Luke 21:7-36; Phil. 3:20-21; I Cor. 1:7; I Thess. 1:10; II Thess. 3:5).

Watchfulness on the part of a Christian indicates faith. He believes his Lord is coming. Therefore he is watching and waiting. Watchfulness indicates a desire for His coming. We are urged to earnestly anticipate "that blessed hope" of the Saviour's return from heaven (Titus 2:13). This anticipation of deliverance gives courage and stedfastness as we fight "the good fight of faith." Alexander Maclaren asks, "If professing Christians lived with the great white throne and the heavens and the earth fleeing away before Him that sits on it, ever burning before their inward eye, how could they wallow amid the mire of animal indulgence?"[1] The answer is that the true believer will "abhor that which is evil; cleave to that which is good" because of the blessing and rewards which Christ will bring with Him (Romans 12:9).

D. *Working.* Paul, in urging Timothy to preach the word faithfully and fully, strives to motivate him first of all by the coming of Christ when He says, "I charge thee therefore before God, and the Lord Jesus Christ, who shall judge the quick and the dead at His appearing and his kingdom, preach the word..." (II Tim. 4:1, 2a).

In the parable of the talents, which Jesus gave in Matthew 25, the motive for using the talents was that the Lord would return and demand a reckoning. The parable of the

1. Blakely, Fred O., *The Apostles' Doctrine*, Volume I, Page 162.

Waiting Servants and of the Wise Steward says, "blessed is that servant whom his Lord when He cometh, shall find so doing" (Luke 12:43). When we stand before the judge of the universe we will want to hear Him say, "Well done." We have no promise that He will say "well done" unless we have done well.

Christians in every generation have looked for and expected Jesus to come in their lifetime. This is as it should be. The anticipation of His coming moves the Christian to live righteously, watch faithfully and work diligently. One day Christ assuredly will come. We must be ready.

Some golden daybreak, Jesus will come;
Some golden daybreak—battles all won;
He'll shout the victory—break through the blue;
Some golden daybreak—for me, for you.

QUESTIONS — THE COMING OF THE LORD

TRUE - FALSE

_____ 1. Very little is said in the New Testament about the second coming.

_____ 2. The Bible says Jesus will come like a thief (unexpectedly).

_____ 3. Christ will be alone when He comes this time.

_____ 4. The righteous dead will be raised at Jesus' coming.

_____ 5. Jesus said that no one but He and the Father knew the time of His return.

_____ 6. Man has not been foolish enough to set a date for Christ's return.

_____ 7. Jesus' return will be a spiritual coming, not a visible one.

_____ 8. Peter prophesied that many would deny that Christ would come again.

_____ 9. The clouds are said to be God's chariot.

_____ 10. There is no need to watch for Christ's return since we do not know when it will be.

THE COMING OF THE LORD

COMPLETE:

1. List three (3) major responses that belief in the second coming motivates.

   a. _____.

   b. _____.

   c. _____.

2. What Christian characteristics should the second coming inspire?

   _____

   _____

   _____

3. List three (3) testimonies to the fact of Christ's return.

   _____

   _____

   _____

4. What will be the manner of His coming?

   _____

   _____

   _____

BIBLIOGRAPHY

Alber, John G., *The Principle of the Tithe.* (Lncoln, Nebraska: Reporter Publishing Company.)

Allen, F. G., *Old Path Pulpit.*

Allen, Roland, *Missionary Methods: St. Paul's or Ours?* (London: World Dominion Press), 1930.

Allen, Roland, *The Spontaneous Expansion of the Church.* (Grand Rapid, Michigan: William B. Eerdman's Publishing Company), 1962.

Blakely, Fred O., *The Apostles' Doctrine Vol. I, II,* (Highland, Indiana), 1959.

Brents, T. W., *Gospel Sermons.* (Nashville: Gospel Advocate Co.)

Campbell, Alexander, *The Christian System.* (Cincinnati: Standard Publishing Company).

Casselman, Arthur V., *Into All the World.* (Philadelphia: The Christian Education Press), 1943.

LESSONS IN CHRISTIAN DOCTRINE

Cole, Glenn Gates, Classified Bible Studies. (Holmesville, Ohio: G. G. Cole publisher.) Out of print.

Cook, Harold R., An Introduction to the Study of Christian Missions. (Chicago, Illinois: The Moody Bible Institute.), 1954.

Davis George T. B., Fulfilled Prophecies that Prove the Bible. (Philadelphia, Pennsylvania: The Million Testaments Campaign), 1931.

DeWelt, Don, The Church and The Bible, College Press, Joplin, Missouri.

Dornette, Ralph, Bible Answers To Popular Questions.

Fisher, George Park, The Grounds of Theistic and Christian Beliefs. (New York: Charles Scribner's Sons), 1921.

Flynn, Leslie B., Your God and Your Gold, (Grand Rapids, Michigan: Zondervan Publishing House), 1961.

Glover Robert Hall, The Bible Basis of Missions. (Los Angeles, California: Bible House of Los Angeles, California), 1946.

Hasting's Dictionary of the Bible.

Hayden, W. L., Church Polity.

Hoven, Victor, Bible Doctrine. (Eugene, Oregan: Northwest Christian College)

Hunt, Julian O., Christian is the Name of the Church (Published by author)

International Standard Bible Encyclopedia. (Grand Rapids; Michigan: William B. Eerdmans Publishing Company).

Johnson, Ashley S., The Great Controversy. (Cincinnati: F. L. Rowe Company).

Johnson, Ashley S., The Life of Trust. (Old Paths Book Club).

Lipscomb and Sewell, Questions Answered. (Nashville: Gospel Advocate Company.)

McGarvey, J. W., Acts of Apostles. (Cincinnati, Ohio: Standard Publishing Co.)

Milligan, Robert, Scheme of Redemption. (St. Louis: Christian Board of Publication).

Murch, James DeForest, Teach Me To Pray. (Cincinnati, Ohio: Standard Publishing Company), 1958.

Pray Without Ceasing, (Scottdale, Pennsylvania: Herald Press).

Scott, Walter, The Gospel Restored. (Rosemead, California: Old Paths Book Club).

Smith, Wilbur M., The Supernaturalness of Christ, (Boston Massachusetts: W. A. Wilde Company), 1954.

Smith, Wilbur M., Therefore Stand. (Boston: W. A. Wilde Company), 1945.

Sweeney, Z. T., New Testament Christianity, Vol. I, II, III, (Columbus, Indiana: New Testament Christianity Book Fund Incorporated), 1930.

Thomas, J. D., Facts and Faith, Vol. I., (Abilene, Texas: Biblical Research Press), 1965.

White, Samuel J., The Bible Self-Explanatory. (Published by Author, Tampa, Fla.)

Winder, F. J., That They May Be Won. (Portland, Oregon: Willamette Printing Co.) 1936.

Zollars, Ely V., The Great Salvation. (Cincinnati: Standard Publishing Co.)